THE
GOSPEL OF
LUKE

Deut 6: 4-5
LOVE

WILLIAM MacDONALD

Emmaus
Correspondence
School

LUKE 24:27

Developed as a study course by Emmaus Correspondence School, founded in 1942.

The Gospel of Luke
William MacDonald

Published by:
Emmaus Correspondence School
(A division of ECS Ministries)
PO Box 1028
Dubuque, IA 52004-1028
phone: (563) 585-2070
email: ecsorders@ecsministries.org
website: www.ecsministries.org

First Printed 1968 (AK '68), 1 UNIT
Revised 1974 (AK '74), 1 UNIT
Revised 2005 (AK '05), 1 UNIT
Reprinted 2008 (AK '05), 1 UNIT
Revised 2011 (AK '11), 2 UNITS
Reprinted 2014 (AK '11), 2 UNITS
Reprinted 2020 (AK '11), 2 UNITS

ISBN 978-0-940293-29-8

Code: LK

Printed in the United States of America

STUDENT INSTRUCTIONS

The skeptic Renan called Luke's gospel "The most beautiful book in the world." And so it is! The Lord Jesus is especially presented to us by Luke as the friend of "publicans and sinners," the outcasts of society.

We see Him breaking the shackles of national prejudice to show His tenderness, compassion, and sympathy to those outside the nation of Israel. We find that women are given frequent and honorable mention, something quite alien to Jewish custom at the time. Luke's evident goal is to present to us Jesus as "the Son of Man" and as the Savior of mankind. A study of this gospel is bound to be a heartwarming experience.

Lessons You Will Study

Course Components

This course has two parts: this study course and the exam booklet.

How To Study

This study has twelve chapters, and each chapter has its own exam. Begin by asking God to help you understand the material. Read the chapter through at least twice, once to get a general idea of its contents and then again, slowly, looking up any Bible references given.

Begin studying immediately, or if you are in a group, as soon as the group begins. We suggest that you keep a regular schedule by trying to complete at least one chapter per week.

Exams

In the exam booklet there is one exam for each chapter (exam 1 covers chapter 1 of the course). Do not answer the questions by what you think or have always believed. The questions are designed to find out if you understand the material given in the course.

After you have completed each chapter, review the related exam and see how well you know the answers. If you find that you are having difficulty answering the questions, review the material until you think you can answer the questions. It is important that you read the Bible passages referenced as some questions may be based on the Bible text.

How Your Exams Are Graded

Your instructor will mark any incorrectly answered questions. You will be referred back to the place in the course where the correct answer is to be found. After finishing this course with a passing average, you will be awarded a certificate.

If you enrolled in a class, submit your exam papers to the leader or secretary of the class who will send them for the entire group to the Correspondence School.

See the back of the exam booklet for more information on returning the exams for grading.

1

THE BIRTH AND BOYHOOD OF JESUS
(1:1–2:52)

Introduction

In the four gospels we have four separate accounts of the life of a Perfect Man. This is one of the greatest proofs of the inspiration of the Scriptures. No mere man could write a *single* biography of a blameless, spotless life. But in the Gospels we have *four* such biographies.

It might seem like unnecessary repetition to have four accounts of the life of the Lord Jesus Christ except that each evangelist presents Him from a different viewpoint: *Matthew,* as King of Israel; *Mark,* as the Perfect Servant; *Luke,* as the Son of Man; and *John,* as the Son of God.

The Gospels do not profess to give a complete account of the entire life of Christ. They contain carefully chosen incidents from His life, mostly taken from the three years of His public ministry, giving the most intensive

The Gospels contain carefully chosen incidents from Christ's life and public ministry.

coverage to His death, burial, and resurrection. The first three gospels do not contain many ringing evangelistic appeals, presenting the way of salvation, but lay the foundation of the gospel in telling of the death, burial, and resurrection of the Lord Jesus.

At times the accounts in the Gospels seem to contradict one another. How should we react when we find these differences? These differences are inspired by God. Instead of being contradictions, they are specially designed by the Spirit of God to bring out spiritual truth of deep significance. Even if we cannot explain all the differences, we believe that they are meaningful. This should drive us to more diligent study.

5

In the Gospels, we find the events are not always listed in the order in which they occurred. It is good to know at the outset that the Spirit of God often groups events according to their moral teaching. Kelly says, "It will be proved, as we proceed, that Luke's is essentially a moral order, and that he classifies the facts, conversations, questions, replies, and discourses of our Lord according to their inward connection, and not the mere outward succession of events, which is in truth the rudest [simplest] and most infantile [elementary] type of record. But to group events together with their causes and consequences, in their moral order, is a far more difficult task for the historian, as distinguished from the mere chronicler. God can cause Luke to do it perfectly."[1]

In Luke's gospel, emphasis is on Jesus as the Son of Man. His humanity is prominent. His prayer life, for example, is referred to more than in any of the other gospel accounts. His sympathy and compassion are mentioned

> In Luke's gospel, emphasis is on Jesus as the Son of Man.

frequently. Perhaps this is why women and children occupy such a prominent place. The gospel of Luke is also known as the missionary gospel. Here the gospel goes out to the Gentiles, and the Lord Jesus is presented as the Savior of the world. Finally, this gospel is a discipleship manual. We trace the pathway of discipleship in the life of our Lord, and hear it expounded in His training of His followers. It is this feature we shall follow particularly in our exposition. In the life of the Perfect Man, we shall find the elements that make up the ideal life for all people. In His incomparable words we shall also find the way of the cross to which He calls us.

As we turn to studying Luke's gospel, may we hear the Savior's call, forsake all, and follow Him. As someone has said, "Obedience is the organ of spiritual knowledge." The meaning of the Scriptures becomes clearer and dearer to us as we enter into the experiences described.

Outline

1. Birth and Childhood of Jesus—The first twelve years (1:1–2:38; 2:41-50).
2. Silent Years in Nazareth (2:39, 40, 51-52).
3. Three Years of Public Ministry (3:1–19:28).
   a. Galilean Ministry (4:14–9:51).
   b. Perean Ministry (10:1–19:28).

4. Last Week—Jerusalem and Vicinity (19:29–23:56).

5. Resurrection and Ascension (24:1-53).

The How and Why of This Gospel (1:1-4)

In his preface, Luke reveals himself as a historian. He describes the source materials to which he had access and the method he followed, and he explains his purpose in writing. From the human standpoint he had two types of source materials: written accounts of Christ's life and oral reports of eyewitnesses of the events in His life.

The written accounts are described in verse 1: "Inasmuch as many have taken in hand to set in order a narrative of those things which have been fulfilled among us . . ." We do not know who these writers were. Matthew and Mark may have been among them, but any others were obviously not inspired. (John wrote at a later date.)

Luke also depended on oral reports. These are referred to in verse 2: "as those who from the beginning were eyewitnesses and ministers of the word delivered them to us." Luke does not claim to be an eyewitness, but he had interviews with those who were. He describes them as "eyewitnesses and ministers of the word." Here he uses "the word" as a Name of Christ, just as John does in his gospel.

The fact that Luke used written and oral accounts does not deny the verbal inspiration of what he wrote. It simply means the Holy Spirit guided him in choosing and arranging his materials. "Luke makes it perfectly clear that the inspired writers were not miraculously freed from the necessity of hard historical research. Inspiration was not God magically transcending human minds and faculties: it was God expressing His will through the dedication of human minds and faculties. It does not supersede the sacred writer's own personality and make him God's machine; it reinforces his personality and makes him God's living witness."[2]

In verse 3 Luke gives a brief statement of his motivation and method: "It seemed good to me also, having had perfect understanding of all things from the very first, to write to you an orderly account, most excellent Theophilus." About his motivation he simply says, "It seemed good to me also." On the human level, there was the quiet conviction that he should write the gospel. We know, of course, that divine constraint was mingled with this human decision.

In his method, he first traces the course of all things accurately from the beginning, writing them down in order. His task involved a careful, scientific investigation of the course of events in our Savior's life. Luke checked the accuracy of his sources, eliminating all that was not historically true and spiritually relevant, then compiled his materials in order as we have them today. When he says he wrote "an orderly account" he does not mean in chronological order, but in a moral or spiritual order. Events are connected by subject matter and moral instruction rather than by time.

Although this gospel and the book of Acts were both addressed to Theophilus, we know little about him. His title "most excellent" suggests he was a government official. His name means *a friend of God*. Probably he was a Christian holding a position of honor and responsibility in the foreign service of the Roman Empire.

Luke's purpose was to give Theophilus a written account confirming the trustworthiness of all he had been taught concerning the Lord Jesus' life and ministry. The written message would grant it stability by preserving it from the inaccuracies of continued oral transmission. Thus verses 1-4 give us a brief but enlightening background into the human circumstances of how this book was written. We know he wrote by inspiration, implying it in the words "from the very first" (v. 3) which could also be translated "from above."

A Godly Couple, Yet Childless (1:5-7)

Luke begins his narrative by introducing the parents of John the Baptist. They lived in Jerusalem when Herod the Great was king of Judea. Herod was an Idumean, a descendant of Esau.

Zacharias (meaning *the Lord remembers*) was a priest belonging to the course of Abijah, one of the twenty-four shifts into which David had divided the Jewish priesthood (1 Chron. 24:10). Each shift served at the temple in Jerusalem twice a year from Sabbath to Sabbath. Because there were so many priests at this time, the privilege of burning incense in the holy place came only once in a lifetime, if at all.

Elizabeth (meaning *the oath of God*) was also a descendant of the priestly tribe of Aaron. She and her husband were devout Jews, scrupulously careful in observing the Old Testament Scriptures, both moral and ceremonial. They were not sinless, but when they did sin they made sure to offer a sacrifice or otherwise to obey the ritualistic requirement. They had no children, a reproachful condition for any Jew. The problem was aggravated because they both were now quite advanced in years.

The Promised Son to be Messiah's Forerunner (1:8-17)

One day Zacharias was performing his priestly duties in the temple. This was a great day in his life because he had been chosen by lot to burn incense in the holy place. The people had gathered outside the temple and were praying. No one seems to know definitely the time signified by "the hour of incense."

> The gospel opens with people praying at the temple and closes with people praising God at the temple.

It is interesting to notice that the gospel opens with people praying at the temple and closes with people praising God at the temple. The intervening chapters tell how prayers were answered in the Person and work of the Lord Jesus.

With priest and people engaged in prayer, it was an appropriate time and setting for a divine revelation. An angel of the Lord appeared at the right side of the altar, the place of favor. At first Zacharias was terrified; none of his contemporaries had ever seen an angel. But the angel reassured him with wonderful news. A baby would be born to Elizabeth to be named John (*the favor, grace, of Jehovah*). Besides bringing joy and gladness to his parents, he would be a blessing to many.

This child would be great in the eyes of the Lord (the only kind of greatness that really matters). First, he would be great in his personal separation to God; he would drink no wine (made from grapes) or strong drink (made from grain). Second, he would be great in his spiritual endowment; he would be filled with the Holy Spirit from the time of his birth. (This does not mean John was saved or converted from birth, only that God's Spirit was in him from the outset preparing him for his special mission as Christ's forerunner.) Third, he would be great in his role as herald of the Messiah, turning many of the Jewish people to the Lord. His ministry would be like Elijah, the prophet, seeking to bring the people into right relationship with God through repentance. "His preaching would turn the hearts of careless parents to a real spiritual concern for their children. Also he would bring back the hearts of disobedient, rebellious children to the 'wisdom of the just."[3] Or, as Ryle has so aptly stated, he would strive to gather out of the world a company of believers who would be ready to meet the Lord in the day of His appearing. This is a worthy ministry for each of us.

Notice how the deity of Christ is implied in verses 16 and 17. Verse 16 says John would turn many of the children of Israel to the Lord their God. Verse 17 says John would go before Him. To whom does the word *Him* refer? Obviously to the "Lord their God" in the preceding verse we know John was the forerunner of Jesus. The inference is clear: Jesus is God.

Zacharias's Unbelief, Dumbness, and Restoration (1:18-25)

Aged Zacharias was struck by the sheer impossibility of the promise. Both he and his wife were too old to become the parents of a child. His plaintive question expressed all the pent-up doubt of his heart.

The angel answered first by introducing himself as Gabriel (man of God). Though commonly described as an archangel, he is mentioned in Scripture as one who stands in the presence of God and brings messages from God to man (Dan. 8:16; 9:21).

> Gabriel stands in the presence of God and brings messages from God to man.

Because Zacharias doubted, he lost the power of speech until the child was born. Whenever a believer entertains doubts concerning what God has said, he loses his testimony and song. Unbelief seals lips, and they remain sealed until faith returns and bursts forth in praise and witness.

Outside, the people were waiting impatiently: ordinarily the priest who was burning incense would have appeared much sooner. When Zacharias finally came out, he had to communicate with them by making signs. Then they realized that he had seen a vision in the temple. After his tour of duty at the temple, he went home, still unable to speak, as the angel had predicted.

When Elizabeth became pregnant she went into seclusion in her home for five months, rejoicing within herself that the Lord had seen fit to free her from the reproach of being childless.

Mary Will Bear the Messiah (1:26-38)

Six months later, the angel reappeared—this time to a virgin named Mary who lived in the city of Nazareth, in the district of Galilee. Mary was engaged to a man named Joseph, a lineal descendant of David, who inherited legal rights to the throne of David, even though he was a carpenter. Then engagement was considered a much more binding contract than today. It could be broken only by a legal decree similar to divorce.

The angel addressed Mary as one who was highly favored, one whom the Lord was visiting with special privilege. Two points should be noted here: (1) The angel did not worship Mary or pray to her: he simply greeted her. (2) He did not say she was "full of grace," but "highly favored" or "favored by grace."

Mary was understandably upset by this greeting; she wondered what it meant. The angel calmed her fears, and then told her that God was choosing her to be the mother of the long-awaited Messiah. Notice the important truths enshrined in the annunciation:

➤ The real humanity of the Messiah: "You will conceive in your womb and bring forth a Son."

➤ His deity and His mission as Savior: "and shall call His name Jesus" (meaning *Jehovah is the Savior*).

➤ His essential greatness: "He will be great," both as to His Person and His work.

➤ His identity as the Son of God: "and will be called the Son of the Highest."

➤ His title to the throne of David: "the Lord God will give Him the throne of His father David." This establishes Him as the Messiah.

➤ His everlasting and universal kingdom: "and He will reign over the house of Jacob forever; and of His kingdom there will be no end." The first four statements obviously refer to Christ's first advent, whereas the remaining three describe His second coming as King of kings and Lord of lords.

Mary's question, "How can this be?" was one of wonder, not doubt. How could she bear a child when she had never had relations with a man? Although the angel did not say so in so many words, the answer was *virgin birth*. It would be a miracle of the Holy Spirit. He would come upon her, and the power of God would overshadow her.

To Mary's problem of "how?" (it seemed impossible by human reckoning), God's answer was "the Holy Spirit." "Therefore, also, that Holy One who is to be born of you will be called the Son of God." Here we have a sublime statement of the incarnation. Mary's Son would be God manifest in the flesh.

The angel then broke the news to Mary that her relative Elizabeth was six months pregnant—she who had been barren. This miracle would reassure Mary that with God, nothing is impossible. In beautiful submission, Mary yielded herself to the Lord for the accomplishment of His wondrous purposes. The angel then left.

Mary Visits Elizabeth (1:39-45)

We are not told why Mary visited Elizabeth at this time. It may have been to avoid the scandal that would inevitably arise in Nazareth when her condition became known. If this is so, then the welcome given by Elizabeth and the kindness shown would have been doubly sweet.

As soon as Elizabeth heard Mary's voice, the baby leaped in her womb—a mysterious, involuntary response of the unborn forerunner to the arrival of the unborn Messiah. The Holy Spirit controlled Elizabeth, guiding her speech and actions.

Three persons in chapter 1 filled with the Holy Spirit are John the Baptist (v. 15), Elizabeth (v. 41) and Zacharias (v. 67).

One of the marks of a Spirit-filled life is speaking in psalms, hymns, and spiritual songs (Eph. 5:18-19). We are not surprised therefore to find three songs in this chapter, and two in the next. Four of these songs are generally known by Latin titles, taken from the first lines: Elizabeth's Salutation (1:42-45); The Magnificat (*it magnifies*) (1:46-55); Benedictus (*blessed*) (1:68-79); Gloria in Excelsis Deo (*glory to God on high*) (2:14); Nunc Dimittis (*now let depart*) (2:29-32).

Speaking by special inspiration, Elizabeth saluted Mary as "the mother of my Lord." There was not a trace of jealousy in her heart, only joy and delight that the unborn baby would be her Lord. Mary was blessed among women because she was given the privilege of bearing the Messiah. The fruit of her womb is blessed; He is Lord and Savior.

Notice the Bible never speaks of Mary as the mother of God. While it is true she was the mother of Jesus, and Jesus is God, it is still a doctrinal absurdity to speak of God as having a mother. Jesus existed from all eternity. Mary was a finite creature with a definite date when she began to exist. She was the mother of Jesus only in His incarnation.

Elizabeth rehearsed the seemingly intuitive excitement of her unborn child when Mary first spoke. Then she assured Mary that her faith would be abundantly rewarded, and her expectation would be fulfilled. She had not believed in vain. Her Baby would be born as promised.

Mary's Song Magnifying the Lord (1:46-56)

The Magnificat resembles Hannah's song (1 Sam. 2:1-10). First, Mary praised the Lord for what He had done for her (vv. 46-49). Notice she said (v. 48) "all generations will *call me blessed*" (emphasis added) She would not be one who conferred blessings, but one who would *be* blessed. It should be noticed she is speaking of God as her Savior, disproving the idea that Mary was sinless. Second, she praised the Lord for His mercy to those who fear Him in every generation. He abases the proud and mighty, and exalts the poor and hungry (vv. 50-53).

> The Bible never speaks of Mary as the mother of God.

Finally, she magnified the Lord for His faithfulness to Israel in keeping the promises He had made to Abraham and his seed (vv. 54-55).

After staying with Elizabeth for three months, Mary returned to Nazareth. She was not yet married. No doubt she became the object of suspicion and slander in the neighborhood. But God would vindicate her; she could afford to wait.

Birth of the Forerunner (1:57-66)

At the appointed time, Elizabeth gave birth to a baby boy. Her relatives and friends were delighted. On the eighth day, when the boy was circumcised, they thought it was a foregone conclusion he would be named Zacharias, after his father. When Elizabeth told them the child's name would be John, they were surprised; none of his relatives had that name.

To get the final decision, they made signs to Zacharias. (This indicates that he was not only dumb, but deaf as well.) Calling for a writing tablet, he settled the matter—the baby's name was John. The people were all surprised. But it was more of a surprise when Zacharias's speech returned as soon as he wrote "John." The news spread quickly through Judea, and people wondered about the future work of this unusual boy. They knew God's special favor was upon him.

Zacharias Prophesies Concerning John (1:67-80)

Freed from the fetters of unbelief and filled with the Holy Spirit, Zacharias was inspired to utter an eloquent hymn of praise. This song is rich in quotations from the Old Testament. It may be outlined as follows:

Praise to God for what He had done (1:68-69). Zacharias realized the birth of his son, John, indicated the imminence of the coming Messiah. He spoke of Christ's advent as an accomplished fact before it happened. Faith enabled him to say God had already visited and brought redemption for His people by sending the Redeemer. Jehovah had raised up a horn of salvation in the royal house of David. (A horn was used to hold the oil for anointing kings; therefore it might mean here a *King* of salvation from the kingly line of David.)

Praise to God for fulfilling prophecy (1:70-71). The coming of the Messiah had been predicted by the holy prophets since the ages began. It would mean salvation and safety from enemies.

Praise to God for His faithfulness to His promises (1:72-75). The Lord had made an unconditional covenant of salvation with Abraham. This promise was fulfilled by the coming of Abraham's seed—the Lord Jesus Christ. The salvation he brought was both external and internal. Externally, it meant deliverance from the hand of enemies. Internally, it meant serving Him with fear, in holiness and righteousness.

G. Campbell Morgan brings out two striking thoughts on this passage[4]. First, the arresting connection between the name of John and the theme of the song—both are the grace of God. Then he finds allusions to the names of John, Zacharias, and Elizabeth in verses 72 and 73 (John—the mercy promised, v. 72: Zacharias—to remember, v. 72; Elizabeth—the oath, v. 73). God's favor, as announced by John, results from His remembering the oath of His covenant.

The mission of John, the Savior's herald (1:76-77), John would be the prophet of the Most High, preparing the hearts of the people for the coming of the Lord, and proclaiming salvation for the people through the forgiveness of their sins. References to Jehovah in the Old Testament are applied to Jesus in the New. Malachi predicted a messenger to prepare the way before Jehovah (3:1). Zacharias identifies John as the messenger. We know that John came to prepare the way before Jesus. The obvious conclusion is that Jesus is Jehovah.

Christ's coming is likened to the sunrise (1:78-79). For centuries, the world had been in darkness. Now through the tender mercy of God, dawn was about to break. It would come in the Person of Christ, shining on the Gentiles who were in darkness and in the shadow of death, and guiding Israel's feet in the path of peace (see Malachi 4:2).

The chapter closes with a simple statement that John grew physically and spiritually, remaining in the wilderness till the day would come for his public appearance to the nation of Israel.

The Birth of Jesus in Bethlehem (2:1-7)

Caesar Augustus made a decree that the whole world should be enrolled; a census should be taken throughout his empire. It was first taken when Quirinius (Cyrenius, AV) was governor of Syria.

For many years, the accuracy of Luke's gospel was called into question because of this reference to Quirinius. But recent archaeological discoveries tend to confirm the record. From Caesar Augustus's view, he was demonstrating supremacy over the Greek-Roman world. But from God's view, this Gentile emperor was merely a puppet to further the divine program (see Proverbs 21:1). Augustus's decree brought Joseph and Mary to Bethlehem at exactly the right time so the Messiah might be born there in fulfillment of prophecy (Micah 5:2).

Bethlehem was crowded when they arrived from Galilee. The only vacant place was the stable of an inn. This was a preview of how men would receive their Savior. It was while there that Mary gave birth to Jesus, her firstborn Son, wrapped Him in swaddling clothes (strips of cloth), and laid Him in a manger. Thus God visited our planet in the Person of a helpless Baby, and in the poverty of an ill-smelling stable.

The Announcement to the Shepherds (2:8-14)

The first intimation of this unique birth was not given to the religious leaders in Jerusalem, but to shepherds on Judean hillsides. "And is there not a world of meaning in the fact that it was very ordinary people, busy about very ordinary tasks, whose eyes first saw the 'glory of the coming of the Lord'? It means, first, that the place of duty, however humble, is the place of vision. And it means, second, that it is the men who have kept to the deep, simple pieties of life and have not lost the child heart to whom the gates of the Kingdom most readily open."[6]

An angel of the Lord came and stood before the shepherds, and a bright, glorious light shone all around them. As they recoiled in terror, the angel comforted them, breaking the news of good tidings of great joy for all people. That very day, in nearby Bethlehem, a Baby had been born—the Savior, Christ the Lord.

Here we have a theology in miniature. First, He is a *Savior,* which is expressed in His name, Jesus. Then He is *Christ,* the Anointed of God, the Messiah of Israel. Finally, He is the *Lord,* God manifest in the flesh.

The angels gave the shepherds a twofold sign. First the Baby would be wrapped in swaddling clothes. They had seen babies in swaddling clothes before (it is still common practice to wrap newborns snugly to restrict their movements), but this Baby was the Lord. The second part of the sign was that He would be lying in a manger. Think of the Creator and Sustainer of the universe entering human history not as a conquering military Hero, but as a little Baby! Yet this is the truth of the incarnation.

Heaven's pent-up ecstasy could not longer be restrained. A multitude of angels from heaven suddenly appeared alongside the first angel, singing praise to God. Their song, known generally by the title, "Gloria in Excelsis Deo," catches up the full significance of the birth of the Baby. His life and ministry would bring glory to God and peace on earth to those to whom He was extending goodwill, that is, to those who would repent of their sins and receive Jesus Christ as Lord and Savior.

The Visit of the Shepherds (2:15-20)

As soon as the angels departed, the shepherds hurried to Bethlehem and found Mary and Joseph, and Jesus lying in the manger. They gave a complete report of the angels' visit, causing considerable surprise among those who had gathered in the stable. But Mary had a deeper understanding of what was going on; she treasured this news, and knowingly pondered it in her heart.

The shepherds returned to their flocks, overjoyed at all they had heard and seen, and overflowing in their worship of God.

The Circumcision and Dedication of Jesus (2:21-24)

At least three different rituals are described in this passage. *First* there was the circumcision of Jesus (a token of the covenant that God made with Abraham) when He was eight days old. On this same day, the Baby was named, according to Jewish custom. The angel had previously instructed Mary and Joseph to call Him Jesus. The *second* ceremony was concerned with the purification of Mary. It took place forty days after the birth of Jesus (see Lev. 12:1-4). Ordinarily parents were supposed to bring a lamb for a burnt offering and a young pigeon or turtledove for a sin offering. But the poor were permitted to bring two young pigeons or turtledoves (Lev. 12:6-8). The fact that Mary brought no lamb, but only two young pigeons, is a reflection of the poverty into which Jesus was born.

> The fact that Mary brought only two young pigeons is a reflection of the poverty into which Jesus was born.

The correct translation of verse 22 is: "And when the days of *their* purification according to the Law of Moses were fulfilled . . . ." This raises the question as to who is meant by "their." Certainly there was no need of purification as far as Jesus Himself was concerned. Some people think that Joseph is thus associated with Mary in the ceremony, but this seems strange in view of the fact that Joseph was not the father of the Child. The *third* ritual was the presentation of Jesus at the temple in Jerusalem. Originally God had decreed that all the firstborn sons of Israel belonged to Him; they were to form the priestly class. Later, He set aside the tribe of Levi to serve as priests. Then the parents were permitted to "buy back" or "redeem" their firstborn son by the payment of five shekels at the dedication of him to the Lord.

Simeon Lives to See the Messiah (2:25-35)

Simeon was one of the godly remnant of Jews waiting for the coming of the Messiah. The Holy Spirit revealed to him that he would not die before seeing God's Christ or Anointed One. "The secret of the Lord is with them that fear Him" (Ps. 25:14). There is a mysterious communication of divine knowledge to those who walk in quiet, contemplative fellowship with God.

Simeon entered the temple area on the very day that Jesus' parents were presenting Him to God. Simeon was supernaturally instructed that this Child was the promised Messiah. Taking Jesus in his arms, he uttered the memorable song now known as *Nunc Dimittis* (Now let . . . depart). Simeon recognized that Jesus would be a light to illuminate the Gentiles (His first advent) and would shine in glory on His people Israel (His second advent, v. 32). He was prepared to die after he had met the Lord Jesus. The sting of death was gone.

The way in which a person reacts to the Savior is a test of his inward motives and affections.

After this initial outburst of praise to God for the Messiah, Simeon spoke prophetically to Mary. The prophecy consisted of four parts: (1) *This Child is destined for the falling and rising of many in Israel.* Those who were arrogant, unrepentant, and unbelieving would fall and be punished. Those who humbled themselves, repented of their sins, and received the Lord Jesus would rise and be blessed. (2) *This Child is destined . . . for a sign which will be spoken against.* There was a special significance connected with the Person of Christ. His very presence on earth proved a tremendous rebuke to sin and unholiness, and thus brought out the bitter animosity of the human heart. (3) *Yes, a sword will pierce through your own soul also.* Simeon was here predicting the grief that would flood Mary's heart when she would witness the crucifixion of her Son (John 19:25). (4) *. . . that the thoughts of many hearts may be revealed.* The way in which a person reacts to the Savior is a test of his inward motives and affections.

Anna, the Prophetess (2:36-39)

Anna the prophetess, like Simeon, was a member of the faithful remnant of Israel waiting for the Messiah's advent. She was of the tribe of Asher (meaning *happy, blessed*), one of the ten tribes carried into captivity by the Assyrians in 721 BC. Anna must have been over one hundred years old, having been married for seven years, then widowed for eighty-four years.

As a prophetess, she undoubtedly received divine revelations and served as a mouthpiece of God. She was faithful in her attendance at the temple's public services, worshipping with fastings and supplications night and day. Age did not deter her from serving the Lord.

As Jesus was being presented to the Lord, and Simeon was speaking to Mary, Anna came up giving thanks to God for the promised Redeemer. Then she spoke about Jesus to the faithful ones in Jerusalem who were expecting redemption. After Joseph and Mary had completed the rites of purification and dedication, they returned to their home in Nazareth.

It will be noticed here that Luke omits any mention of the visit of the wise men or of the flight into Egypt (see Matthew chapters 1 and 2).

The Early Years of Jesus (2:40-52)

The normal growth of Jesus is set forth in verse 40. *Physically* He grew and became strong. He passed through the usual stages of physical development, learning to walk, talk, play, and work. Because of this He can sympathize with us in every stage of our growth. *Mentally*, He was filled with wisdom. He not only learned His ABCs, His numbers, and all the common knowledge of that day, but He grew in wisdom, that is, in the practical application of this knowledge to the problems of life. *Spiritually* the favor of God was upon Him. He walked in fellowship with God and in dependence on the Holy Spirit. He studied the Scriptures, spent time in prayer, and delighted to do His Father's will.

A Jewish boy becomes a man and a son of the law at the age of twelve. When Jesus was twelve years old, His family made their annual pilgrimage to Jerusalem for His first Passover. But when they left to return to Galilee, they didn't notice that Jesus was not in the company. This may seem strange to us unless we realize that the family probably traveled with a fairly large caravan. They no doubt assumed that Jesus was walking with others of His own age.

Before condemning Joseph and Mary, remember how easy it is for us to travel a day's journey, supposing Jesus to be in the company, when actually we have lost contact with Him through unconfessed sin in our lives. To re-establish contact with Him, we must go back to the place where fellowship was broken, then confess and forsake our sin.

Returning to Jerusalem, the distraught parents found Jesus in the temple. He was sitting among the teachers listening and asking questions. There is no suggestion of His acting as a precocious child, disputing with His elders. He, as a normal child, was learning in humility and quietness from His teachers. Yet in the course of the proceedings, He must have been asked some questions, because the people were amazed by His knowledge and His answers.

His parents also were astonished when they found Jesus participating intelligently in a discussion with those much older than He. Yet His mother expressed her accumulated anxiety and irritation by reproving Him. Didn't He know they had been worried about Him? The Lord's answer (v. 49) shows He was fully aware of His identity as the Son of God, and of His divine mission. "Why did you seek me? Did you not know that I must be about My Father's business?" She said, "*Your father* and I . . . ." He said, "*My Father's* business." At the time, they did not understand what He meant by His cryptic remark.

Reunited, they returned to Nazareth. The moral excellence of Jesus is seen in the words "He was subject unto them." Although He was the Creator of the universe, He took His place as an obedient child in this humble Jewish family. And all the time, Mary was pondering His sayings in her heart.

In verse 52, we have the true humanity and normal growth of our Lord depicted: His *mental* growth—increased in wisdom: His *physical* growth—and stature; His *spiritual* growth—in favor with God and His *social* growth—in favor with man. He was absolutely perfect in every aspect of His growth.

Here Luke skips silently over eighteen years that the Lord Jesus spent in Nazareth as the Son of a carpenter. These years teach us the importance of preparation and training, the need for patience, and the value of common work. They warn against the temptation to jump from spiritual birth to public ministry. Those who do not have a normal spiritual childhood and adolescence court disaster in their later life and testimony.

1 William Kelly, *An Exposition of the Gospel of Luke* (London: Pickering and Inglis, n.d.) p. 16.
2 James S. Stewart. *The Life and Teaching of Jesus Christ* (New York: Abingdon Press. n.d.) p. 9.
3 G. Coleman Luck, *Luke* (Chicago: Moody Press, 1960) p. 17.
4 G. Campbell Morgan, *The Gospel According to Luke* (New York: Fleming H. Revell Co., 1931) pp. 30, 31.
5 J. N. Darby, *Synopsis of the Books of the Bible*, Vol. III (New York: Gospel Book and Tract Depot, n.d.) p. 293.
6 James S. Stewart, *op. cit.*, p. 24.

2

JESUS BEGINS HIS MINISTRY

(3:1–4:44)

John, the Baptist, Begins His Ministry (3:1-6)

L uke identifies the year John began to preach by naming the political and religious leaders who were then in power: one emperor, one governor, three tetrarchs, and two high priests. The political rulers mentioned show with what an iron grip the nation of Israel was held in subjugation. The fact that there were two high priests in Israel (when the Mosaic Law required just one) indicates the nation was in disorder religiously as well as politically.

— ✺ —

John the Baptist was a true prophet, an embodied conscience crying out against sin and calling for spiritual renewal.

— ✺ —

Though these were great men in the world's estimation, they were wicked, unscrupulous men in God's eyes. When He wanted to speak to the people, therefore, He by-passed the palace and the synagogue and sent His word to them via John, the son of Zacharias, out in the desert. John immediately traveled to the region of the Jordan River, probably near Jericho. There he called upon the nation of Israel to repent of its sins in order to receive forgiveness in preparation for the coming of the Messiah. He also called upon the people to be baptized as an outward sign of repentance. John was a true prophet, an embodied conscience crying out against sin and calling for spiritual renewal.

His ministry was in fulfillment of the prophecy in Isaiah 40:3-5. He was a voice crying in the wilderness. Spiritually speaking, Israel was a wilderness at this time. As a nation, it was dry and cheerless, bringing forth no fruit for God. To be ready for the coming of the Lord, the people had to undergo a moral change.

When a king was going to make a royal visit in those days, elaborate preparations were made to smooth the highways and to make his approach as direct as possible. This is what John was calling the people to do, by preparing their own hearts to receive Him.

The effects of Christ's coming are described in verses 5 and 6. Every valley would be filled—those who are truly repentant and humble would be saved and satisfied. Every mountain and hill will be brought low—people like the scribes and Pharisees who were haughty and arrogant would be humbled. The crooked will be made straight—those who were dishonest, like the tax-gatherers, would have their characters straightened out. The rough ways will be made smooth—soldiers and others with rough, crude temperaments would be tamed and refined. A final result will be that all flesh, both Jews and Gentiles, would see the salvation of God. In His first advent the offer of salvation went to all men, though not all received Him. When He comes to reign, this verse will have its complete fulfillment. Then all Israel will be saved, and the Gentiles too will share in the blessings of His glorious kingdom.

People Are Called to Repentance (3:7-14)

When a multitude of people came out to John for baptism, he realized they were not all sincere. Some were mere pretenders, with no hunger or thirst for righteousness. It was these whom John addressed as offspring of serpents. The question, "Who warned you to flee from the wrath to come?" implies that John had not done so; his message was addressed to those who were willing to confess their sins.

If they really meant business with God they should show true repentance by manifesting a transformed life. Genuine repentance produces fruit. They should not start thinking that their descent from Abraham was sufficient; relationship to godly people does not make men godly. God was not limited to the human descendants of Abraham to carry out His purposes; He could take the stones by the River Jordan and raise up children to Abraham. Stones here are probably a picture of Gentiles whom God could transform by a miracle of divine grace into believers with faith like that of Abraham. This is exactly what happened. The human descendants of Abraham, as a nation, rejected the Christ of God. But Gentiles received Him as Lord and

Savior, thus becoming the spiritual seed of Abraham.

The ax lying at the root of the trees is a figurative expression, meaning Christ's coming would test the reality of man's repentance. Those individuals who did not manifest the fruits of repentance would be condemned. "John's words and phrases went from his mouth like swords: 'generation of vipers,' 'wrath to come,' 'ax,' 'cut down,' 'thrown into the fire.' The Lord's prophets were never mealy-mouthed: they were great moralists, and often their words came crashing upon the people as the battle-axes of our forefathers upon the helmets of their foes."[1]

Stung with conviction, the people asked John for some practical suggestions of how to demonstrate the reality of their repentance. In verses 11-14, he gave them specific ways of how to prove their sincerity. In general, they should love their neighbors as themselves by sharing their clothing and food with the poor. As for the tax-collectors, they should be strictly honest in all their dealings. Since they as a class were notoriously crooked, this would be a very definite evidence of reality. Finally, soldiers on active duty were told to avoid three sins that were common to men in the military: extortion, slander, and discontent. Of course men were not saved by doing these things; these were the outward evidences that their hearts were truly right before God.

The Baptist Exalts the Messiah (3:15-17)

John's humility was remarkable. He compared himself in a self-depreciating way with Christ, explaining his baptism was outward and physical, whereas Christ's would be inward and spiritual. He stated he was not worthy to untie the Messiah's shoelace. Christ's baptism would be "with the Holy Spirit and with fire": a two-fold ministry. First, He would baptize believers with the Holy Spirit--a promise that took place on the day of Pentecost when believers were baptized into the body of Christ. Second, He would baptize with fire, a symbol of judgment. In the following verse the Lord is pictured as a winnower of grain. As He shovels the grain into the air, the chaff is blown to the sides of the threshing floor. Then it is swept up and burned. When John was speaking to a mixed multitude—believers and unbelievers—he mentioned both the baptism of the Spirit and fire (Matthew 3:11 and here). When speaking to believers only (Mark 1:5), he omitted the baptism of fire (Mark 1:8). No true believer will ever experience the baptism of fire.

Herod Imprisons John (3:18-20)

Luke now turns the spotlight from John to Jesus, summarizing the remainder of John's ministry, and carries us forward to the time of his imprisonment by Herod.

John's imprisonment actually took place about eighteen months later. He had reproved Herod for living in an adulterous relationship with his sister-in-law.

Baptism of Jesus (3:21-22)

As John retires from our attention, the Lord Jesus moves out into the position of prominence. He opens His public ministry at about the age of thirty by being baptized in the River Jordan.

> The prayer life of our Lord is a dominant theme in this gospel.

There are several points of interest in this account of His baptism: First, all three Persons of the Trinity are found here: Jesus (v. 21); the Holy Spirit (v. 22a); the Father (v. 22b). Second, Luke alone records the fact that Jesus prayed at His baptism (v. 21). This is in keeping with Luke's aim to present Christ as the Son of Man, ever dependent on God the Father. The prayer life of our Lord is a dominant theme in this gospel. He prayed here, at the outset of His public ministry. He prayed when He was becoming well known and when crowds were following Him (5:16). He spent a whole night in prayer before choosing the twelve disciples (6:12). He prayed prior to the incident at Caesarea Philippi, the high-water mark of His teaching ministry (9:18). He prayed on the Mount of Transfiguration (9:28). He prayed in the presence of His disciples, and this called forth a discourse on prayer (11:1). He prayed for backsliding Peter (22:32). He prayed in the garden of Gethsemane (22:41, 44). Third, Jesus' baptism is one of three times when God spoke from heaven in connection with the ministry of His own dear Son. For thirty years the eye of God had examined that flawless Life in Nazareth; here His verdict was, "I am well pleased."

The other two times when the Father publicly spoke from heaven were when Peter suggested building three tabernacles on the Mount of Transfiguration (Luke 9:35), and when the Greeks came to Philip, desiring to see Jesus (John 12:20-28).

The Genealogy of Jesus (3:23-38)

Before taking up the public ministry of our Lord, Luke pauses to give His genealogy. If Jesus is truly human, then He must be descended from Adam; this genealogy demonstrates that He was.

Generally it is believed this gives the genealogy of Jesus through the line of Mary. Advocates of this view point out that verse 23 does not say that Jesus was the son of Joseph, but "(as was supposed) the son of Joseph." If this view is correct, then Heli (v. 23) was the father-in-law of Joseph and the father of Mary.

Why do scholars believe this is the Lord's genealogy through Mary?

1. The most obvious reason is that Joseph's family line is traced in Matthew's gospel (1:2-16).

2. In the early chapters of Luke's gospel, Mary is more prominent than Joseph, but it is the reverse in Matthew.

3. Women's names were not commonly used among the Jews as genealogical links. This would account for the omission of Mary's name.

4. In Matthew 1:16, it distinctly states that Jacob begat Joseph. Here in Luke, it does not say that Heli begat Joseph; it says Joseph was the son of Heli. Son may mean son-in-law.

5. In the original language, the definite article (*tou*) in the genitive form ("of the") appears before every name in the genealogy except one—Joseph. This singular exception strongly suggests Joseph was included only because of his marriage to Mary.

Although it is not necessary to examine the genealogy in detail, it is helpful to note several important points:

1. This list shows Mary was descended from David through his son Nathan (v. 31). In Matthew's gospel, Jesus inherited the legal right to the throne of David through Solomon.

   As legal son of Joseph, the Lord fulfilled that part of God's covenant with David promising him his throne would continue forever. But Jesus could not have been the real son of Joseph without coming under God's curse on Jeconiah, which decreed that none of his descendants would prosper (Jer. 22:30).

   As the real son of Mary, Jesus fulfilled that part of God's covenant with David promising him his seed would sit upon his throne forever. Nathan, another of David's sons, wasn't under the curse that was pronounced on Jeconiah.

2. Adam is described as the son of God (v. 38). This means simply that he was created by God.

3. It seems obvious the Messianic line ended with the Lord Jesus. No one else can ever present valid legal claim to the throne of David.

The Temptation of Jesus (4:1-13)

There never was a time in our Lord's life when He was not full of the Holy Spirit, but it is specifically mentioned here in connection with His temptation. To be full of the Holy Spirit means to be completely yielded to Him and to be completely obedient to every word of God. A man who is full of the Spirit is emptied of known sin and of self and is richly indwelt by the Word of God.

> A man who is full of the Spirit is emptied of known sin and of self and is richly indwelt by the Word of God.

As Jesus was returning from the Jordan, where He had been baptized, the Spirit directed Him to the wilderness, probably the Wilderness of Judea, along the west coast of the Dead Sea. There the devil tempted Him for forty days—days in which our Lord ate no food. At the end of the forty days came the threefold temptation with which we are familiar. Actually they took place in three different places: the wilderness, a mountain, and the temple in Jerusalem.

Jesus' true humanity is reflected by the words "He was hungry" (v. 2), the target of the first temptation. Satan suggested the Lord should use His divine power to satisfy bodily hunger. The subtlety was that the act in itself was perfectly legitimate. But it would have been wrong for Jesus to do it in obedience to Satan; He must act in accordance with the will of His Father.

Jesus did not argue but resisted the temptation by quoting Scripture (Deut. 8:3). More important than the satisfaction of physical appetite is obedience to God's Word. "A single text silences when used in the power of the Spirit. The whole secret of strength in conflict is using the Word of God in the right way" (J. N. Darby).

In the second temptation, the devil showed Jesus all the kingdoms of the world in a moment of time. It doesn't take long for Satan to show all he has to offer. Notice the world itself was not offered, but the *kingdoms* of this world. There is a sense in which Satan does have authority over the kingdoms of this world. Man's sin has made Satan "the prince of this world" (John 12:31; 14:30; 16:11), "the god of this world" (2 Cor. 4:4), and "the prince of the power of the air" (Eph. 2:2). God purposed the kingdoms of this world will one day become the kingdoms of our Lord, and of His Christ (Rev. 11:15). So Satan was offering Christ what would eventually be His anyway. But there could be no short cut to the Throne; the cross had to come first. In the counsels of God, the Lord Jesus had to suffer before He could enter into His glory. He could not ascend to the Throne until first He had ascended the altar. He would not achieve a legitimate end by a wrong means. Under no circumstances would He worship the devil, no matter what the prize might be. Therefore, the Lord quoted Deuteronomy 6:13 showing that as a Man He should worship and serve God alone.

In the third temptation, Satan took Jesus to a pinnacle of the temple in Jerusalem, suggesting He cast Himself down. Had not God promised in Psalm 91:11-12 that He would preserve the Messiah?

Perhaps Satan was tempting Jesus to present Himself as Messiah by performing a sensational stunt. Malachi had predicted the Messiah would suddenly come to His temple (Mal. 3:1). Here then was Jesus' opportunity to obtain fame and notoriety as the promised Deliverer without going to Calvary. For the third time, Jesus resisted temptation by quoting from the Bible. Deuteronomy 6:16 forbade putting God to the test. Repulsed by the sword of the Spirit, Satan left Jesus for a season. Temptations usually come in spasms rather than in streams.

Several additional points should be mentioned in connection with the temptation: (1) The order in Luke differs from that in Matthew. The second and third temptations are reversed; the reason is not clear. (2) In all three cases, the end held out was right enough, but the means was wrong. It is always wrong to obey Satan, to worship him or any other created being. It is wrong to tempt God. (3) The first temptation concerned the body, the second the soul, the third the spirit. They appealed respectively to the lust of the flesh, the lust of the eyes, and the pride of life. (4) These revolve around three of the strongest drives of human existence: physical appetite, desire for power and possessions, and desire for public recognition. How often disciples are tempted to choose a pathway of comfort and ease, to seek a prominent place in the world, and to gain a high position in the church. (5) In all three temptations, Satan used religious language and thus clothed the temptations with a garb of outward respectability. He even quoted Scripture (vv. 10-11).

"The study of the temptation narrative illuminates two important points. On the one hand, it proves that temptation is not necessarily sin. On the other hand, the narrative illuminates the great saying of a later disciple—'In that He Himself has suffered, being tempted, He is able to aid those who are tempted' (Hebrews 2:18)."[2]

Sometimes it is suggested that the temptation would have been meaningless if Jesus was not able to sin. The fact is that Jesus is God, and God cannot sin. The Lord Jesus never relinquished any of the attributes of deity. His deity was veiled during His life on earth but it was not and could not be laid aside.

Some say as God He could not sin but as Man He could sin. But He is still both God and Man, and it is unthinkable He could sin today. The purpose of the temptation was not to see if He would sin but to prove that He could not sin. Only a holy, sinless man could be our Redeemer.

Jesus Returns to Galilee (4:14-15)

Between verses 13 and 14 there is a gap of about one year. During this time the Lord ministered in Judea. The only record of this ministry is in John 2–5.

When Jesus returned to Galilee for the second year of His public ministry, His fame spread through the entire region.

The Announcement in Nazareth (4:16-21)

In Nazareth, His boyhood town, Jesus regularly went to the synagogue on the Sabbath day, that is, Saturday. There were two other things that we read that He did regularly: He prayed regularly (Luke 22:39), and He made it a habit to teach others (Mark 10:1).

On one visit to the synagogue He rose to read from the Old Testament Scriptures and was handed the scroll on Isaiah's prophecy. The Lord unrolled the scroll to what we now know as Isaiah 61, and read verse 1 and the first half of verse 2. This has always been acknowledged as a description of the ministry of the Messiah. When Jesus said, "Today this Scripture is fulfilled in your hearing," He was saying as clearly as possible that He was the Messiah of Israel.

Notice the revolutionary implications of the Messiah's mission. He came to deal with the enormous problems that have afflicted mankind throughout history: *Poverty,* to preach the gospel to the poor. *Bondage,* to preach deliverance to the captives. *Suffering,* and recovering of sight to the blind. *Oppression,* to set at liberty them that are bruised (oppressed).

In short, He came to preach the acceptable year of the Lord—the dawning of a new era for this world's sighing, sobbing multitudes. He presented Himself as the answer to all the ills by which we are tormented. Whether these ills are thought of in a physical sense or in a spiritual sense, Christ is the answer.

> **The present age of grace is the accepted time and the day of salvation.**

It is significant He stopped reading with the words ". . . to proclaim the acceptable year of the Lord." He did not add the rest of the words from Isaiah ". . . and the day of vengeance of our God." The purpose of His first coming was to preach the acceptable year of the Lord. This present age of grace is the accepted time and the day of salvation. When He returns to earth the second time, it will be to proclaim the day of vengeance of our God. Note the acceptable time is spoken of as a year, the vengeance time as a day.

Jesus Predicts Israel's Rejection and Is Cast Out (4:22-30)

The people were obviously impressed. They spoke well of Him, having been attracted by His gracious words. It was a mystery to them how the son of Joseph, the carpenter, had developed so well.

The Lord knew this popularity was shallow. There was no real appreciation of His true identity or worth. To them, He was just one of their own hometown boys who had made good in Capernaum. He anticipated that they would say to Him, "Physician, heal yourself." Ordinarily this parable would mean, "Do for yourself what you have done for others. Cure your own condition, since you claim to cure others." But here the meaning is slightly different. It is explained as follows: ". . . whatever we have heard done in Capernaum, do also here in Your country," that is, in Nazareth. It was a scornful challenge for Him to perform miracles in Nazareth as He had done elsewhere, and thus save Himself from ridicule.

The Lord replied by stating a deep-rooted principle in human affairs: great men are not appreciated in their own neighborhood. He then cited two pointed incidents in the Old Testament where prophets of God were not appreciated by the people of Israel and so were sent to Gentiles. When there was famine in Israel, Elijah was not sent to any Jewish widows (though there were plenty of them) but to a Gentile widow in Sidon. And although there were many lepers in Israel when Elisha was ministering, he was not sent to any of them. Instead he was sent to the Gentile Naaman, captain of the Syrian army. Imagine the impact of Jesus' words on Jewish minds. They placed women, Gentiles, and lepers at the bottom of the social scale. But here the Lord pointedly placed all three *above* unbelieving Jews.

He was saying that Old Testament history was about to repeat itself. In spite of His miracles, He would be rejected by the city of Nazareth and the nation of Israel. He would then turn to the Gentiles, just as Elijah and Elisha had done.

The people of Nazareth understood exactly what He meant. They were infuriated by the mere suggestion of favor being shown to Gentiles. "Man bitterly hates the doctrine of the sovereignty of God which Christ had just declared. God was under no obligation to work miracles among them."[3]

The people drove Him out of the city to the brow of a hill, intending to throw Him over the precipice. Doubtless this was instigated by Satan as another attempt to destroy the royal seed. But Jesus miraculously walked through the crowd and left the city. His enemies were powerless to stop Him. As far as we know, He never returned to Nazareth.

Demoniac Healed in Capernaum (4:31-37)

The people in Capernaum recognized His teaching was authoritative. His words were convicting and impelling.

Verses 31-41 describe a typical Sabbath day in the Lord's life. He is revealed as Master over demons and disease. First He went to the synagogue, and there met a man with an unclean demon. The adjective "unclean" is often used to describe evil spirits. It means spirits are impure and produce impurity in the lives of their victims.

The reality of demon possession is seen in this passage. First there was a cry of terror—not "Let us alone" (AV) but a terrified Ah-h-h-h! Then the spirit showed clear knowledge that Jesus was the Holy One of God who would eventually destroy the hosts of Satan. Jesus issued a twofold command to the demon. "Be quiet, and come out of him!" The demon did so, after throwing the man to the ground but leaving him unharmed.

The people were amazed! What was different about Jesus' words that unclean spirits obeyed Him? What was that indefinable authority and power with which He spoke! No wonder reports about Him spread throughout the surrounding region.

All the physical miracles of Jesus are pictures of similar miracles He performs in the spiritual realm.

All the physical miracles of Jesus are pictures of similar miracles He performs in the spiritual realm. For instance, the following miracles in Luke's gospel convey these spiritual lessons:

➤ **Casting out unclean spirits** (4:31-37): deliverance from the filth and defilement of sin.

➤ **Healing Peter's mother-in-law of fever** (4:38-39): relief from the restlessness and debility caused by sin.

➤ **Healing of the leper** (5:12-16): restoration from the loathsomeness and hopelessness of sin (see also 17:11-19).

➤ **The palsied man** (5:17-26): freedom from the paralysis of sin and enablement to serve God.

➤ **The widow's son raised to life** (7:11-17): sinners are dead in trespasses and sins, and need life (see also 8:49-56).

➤ **The stilling of the storm** (8:22-26): Christ can control the storms that rage in the lives of His disciples.

➤ **Legion, the demoniac** (8:26-39): sin produces violence and insanity and ostracizes men from decent society. Jesus brings decency and sanity, and fellowship with Himself.

➤ **The woman who touched the hem of His garment** (8:43-48): the impoverishment and depression brought on by sin.

➤ **Feeding of the 5,000** (9:10-17): a sinful world starving for the bread of God. Christ satisfies the need through His disciples.

> ➢ **The demon-possessed son** (9:37-43a): the cruelty and violence of sin, and the healing power of Christ.

> ➢ **The woman with the spirit of infirmity** (13:10-17): sin deforms and cripples, but the touch of Jesus brings perfect restoration.

> ➢ **The man with dropsy** (14:1-6): sin produces discomfort, distress and danger.

> ➢ **Blind beggar** (18:35-43): sin blinds men to eternal realities. The new birth results in opened eyes.

Simon's Mother-in-law Healed (4:38-39)

Next Jesus made a sick-call at Simon's home, where Simon's mother-in-law was ill with a high fever. As soon as the Lord rebuked the fever, it left her. The cure was not only immediate but complete, since she was able to get up and to serve the household. Usually a great fever leaves a person weak and listless.

Advocates of a celibate priesthood find little comfort in this passage. Peter was a married man.

Christ's Power Over Diseases and Demons (4:40-41)

As the Sabbath day drew to a close, the people were freed from enforced inactivity. They brought a great number of invalids and demoniacs to Him. He healed every one and cast out the demons. Many of those who profess to be faith healers today confine their miracles to pre-chosen candidates. Jesus healed *every one* of them.

The expelled demons knew that Jesus was the Son of God. But He would not accept the testimony of demons. They must be silenced. They knew He was the Messiah, but God had other and better instruments to announce the fact.

Jesus Preaches in Cities of Galilee (4:42-44)

The next day, Jesus retired to a lonely place near Capernaum. The crowds kept looking till they found Him, urging Him not to leave. But He reminded them that He had work to do in the other cities of Galilee. So from synagogue to synagogue, He went preaching the good news about the kingdom of God. Jesus Himself was the King. He desired to reign over them. But first they must repent. He would not reign over a people who clung to their sins. This was the obstacle. They wanted to be saved from political problems but not from their sins.

[1] Daily Notes of the Scripture Union.
[2] James S. Stewart, *op. cit.,* p. 45.
[3] John Charles Ryle, *Expository Thoughts on the Gospels, St. Luke*, Vol. I (New York: Fleming H. Revell Co., 1858) p. 121.

3

JESUS CALLS HIS DISCIPLES
(5:1–6:49)

Jesus Calls Simon Peter (5:1-11)

Several important lessons emerge from this simple account of the call of Peter. Jesus used Peter's boat as a pulpit from which to teach the multitude. If we yield all our property and possessions to the Savior, it is wonderful how He uses them, and rewards us too. He told Peter exactly where to find plenty of fish—after Peter and the others had tried all night without success. The omniscient Lord knows where the fish are running. Service carried on by our own wisdom and strength is futile. The secret of success in Christian work is to be guided by Him. Though an experienced fisherman himself, Peter accepted advice from a Carpenter, and as a result, the nets were filled. ". . . at Your word I will let down the net." This shows the value of humility, of teachability, and of implicit obedience. The nets began to break and the ships began to sink (vv. 6-7). Christ-directed service produces problems, but they are worth the trouble. This vision of the glory of the Lord Jesus produced in Peter an overpowering sense of his own unworthiness. It was so with Isaiah (6:5); it is so with all who see the King in His beauty.

Service carried on by our own wisdom and strength is futile.

It was while Peter was engaged in his ordinary employment that Christ called him to be a fisher of men. While you are waiting for guidance, do whatever your hand finds to do. Do it with all your might as unto the Lord. Just as a rudder guides a ship only when it is in motion, so God guides men when they too are in motion. Christ called Peter from catching fish to catching men.

What are all the fish in the ocean compared to the incomparable privilege of seeing one soul won of Christ and for eternity! Peter, James, and John pulled their boats up on the beach and gave everything up to follow Jesus. How much hung on their decision!

A Leper Healed (5:12-16)

Doctor Luke makes special mention of the fact that this man was "full of leprosy," an advanced case and quite hopeless, humanly speaking. The leper's faith was remarkable. He said, ". . . You can make me clean." He had absolute confidence in the power of the Lord Jesus.

When he said, "if You are willing," he was not expressing doubt as to Christ's willingness, but was coming as a suppliant, with no inherent right to be healed, casting himself on the mercy and grace of the Lord.

To touch a leper was dangerous medically, defiling religiously, and degrading socially. But Jesus contracted no defilement. Instead, there surged into the body of the leper an immediate cure; "immediately the leprosy left him." Imagine what it would mean to be hopeless and helpless as a leper and suddenly to be made completely whole. Jesus charged him to tell no one about the cure. He did not want to attract a crowd of curiosity-seekers, or to stir up a popular movement to make Him king. Instead the Lord commanded the leper to go to the priest and present the offering prescribed by Moses (Lev. 13:49; 14:2ff). Every detail of the offering spoke of Christ.

It was the priest's function to examine the leper and determine if he had actually been healed. The priest could not heal; all he could do was pronounce a man healed. The priests had never seen a cleansed leper before. The sight was unique; it should have made them realize that the Messiah had at last appeared, but their hearts were blinded by unbelief.

In spite of the Lord's instructions not to publicize the miracle, the news traveled quickly, and a great crowd came to Him for healing. Afterwards Jesus retired to the desert for a time of prayer. Our Savior was a Man of prayer. It is fitting that this gospel, which presents Him as Son of Man, should have more to say about His prayer life than any other.

Healing of the Palsied Man Provokes Dispute (5:17-26)

As the news of Jesus' ministry spread, the Pharisees and lawyers (teachers of the law) became increasingly hostile. This passage shows them assembling in Galilee with the obvious purpose of finding some accusation against Him.

The power of the Lord was present to heal the sick. Jesus always had the power to heal, but the circumstances were not always favorable. In Nazareth, for instance, He could not do many mighty works because of the unbelief of the people (Matt. 13:58).

Four men brought a paralytic on a small bed to the house where Jesus was teaching. They could not get to Him because of the crowd, so they climbed the outside stairs to the roof. Then they lowered the man through an opening in the roof. Jesus took notice of their faith for going to such lengths to bring a needy person to His attention. He said to the palsied man, "Your sins are forgiven." This unprecedented statement aroused the Pharisees and scribes. They knew no one but God could forgive sins. They were unwilling to admit that Jesus was God, and considered His statement blasphemy. *Dk. Barbstein needs this stolena*

Jesus proceeded to prove to them that He had actually forgiven the man's sins. First He asked them if it were easier to say, "Your sins are forgiven you," or to say, "Rise up and walk." In one sense it is just as easy to *say* one as the other, but it is another thing to do either, since both are humanly impossible. The point here is that it is easier to say, "Your sins are forgiven you," because there is no way of telling if it has happened. If you say, "Rise up and walk," then it is easy to see if the patient has been healed.

> The title, *the Son of Man*, emphasizes the Lord's perfect humanity.

The Pharisees could not *see* that the man's sins had been forgiven, so they would not believe. Therefore, Jesus performed a miracle they could *see*, to prove He had truly forgiven the man's sins. He gave the paralytic the power to walk, "that you may know that the Son of Man has power on earth to forgive sins." The title, *the Son of Man*, emphasizes the Lord's perfect humanity. In one sense, we are all sons of man, but this title "the Son of Man" sets Jesus off from every other man who ever lived. It describes Him as a Man in God's terms as One who is morally perfect, One who would suffer, bleed and die, and One to whom universal headship has been given.

In obedience to His word, the paralyzed man got up, carried his small sleeping pad, and went home praising God. The crowd was literally amazed, and they too glorified God, acknowledging they had seen incredible things that day, the pronouncing of forgiveness and a miracle proving it.

Jesus Calls Levi (5:27-28)

Levi was a Jewish tax collector for the Roman government. Jews hated tax collectors because of collaboration with Rome and their dishonest practices.

One day, while Levi was at work, Jesus passed by and invited him to become His follower. With amazing promptness, Levi forsook all, rose up, and followed. Think of the tremendous consequences flowing from his simple decision. Levi (also known as Matthew) became the writer of the first gospel. It "pays" to hear Christ's call and follow Him.

Levi's Feast and the Pharisees' Questions (5:29-39)

It has been suggested that Levi had three purposes in arranging this great feast: he wanted to honor the Lord; he wanted to witness publicly to his new allegiance; and he wanted to introduce his friends to Jesus.

> Most Jews would not have eaten with a group of "tax collectors and sinners," but Jesus did.

Most Jews would not have eaten with a group of "tax collectors and sinners," but Jesus did. He did not, of course, participate with them in their sins, or do anything to compromise His testimony, but He used these occasions to teach, rebuke, and bless.

When the Pharisees and their scribes (that is, the scribes who were of the orthodox faith) criticized Him for associating with these despised people, Jesus answered that His action was in perfect accord with His purpose in coming into the world. Healthy people do not need a doctor; only those who are sick do. The Pharisees considered themselves to be righteous. They had no deep sense of sin or of need. Therefore, they could not benefit from the ministry of the Great Physician. But more often, tax collectors and sinners realized they needed to be saved from their sins. It was for people like them that the Savior came. Actually, of course, the Pharisees were not righteous. They needed to be saved as much as the tax collectors. But they were unwilling to confess their sins and acknowledge their guilt. So they criticized the Doctor for going to people who were seriously ill.

Their next tactic was to interrogate Jesus on the custom of fasting. After all, the disciples of John the Baptist had followed the ascetic life of their master. And the followers of the Pharisees observed various ceremonial fasts. But Jesus' disciples did not. Why not? The Lord answered, there was no reason for His disciples to fast while He was still with them. He here associates fasting with sorrow and mourning. When He would be taken violently from them by death, they would fast as an expression of their grief.

The three following parables teach a new dispensation had begun, and there could be no mixing of the new and the old. In the first parable, the old garment speaks of the legal system or dispensation, while the new garment pictures the era of grace. They are incompatible. An attempt to mix law and grace results in a spoiling of both. A patch taken from a new garment spoils the new one, and it doesn't match the old one, either in appearance or strength. "Jesus would do no such thing as tack on Christianity to Judaism. Flesh and law go together, but grace and law, God's righteousness and man's, will never mix" (J. N. Darby).

The second parable teaches the folly of putting new wine in old wine skins. The fermenting action of new wine causes pressure on the skins so they are no longer pliable enough or elastic enough to bear. They burst and the wine is spilled. The outmoded forms, ordinances, traditions, and rituals of Judaism were too rigid to hold the joy, exuberance and energy of the new dispensation. The new wine is seen here in the unconventional methods of the four men who brought the paralytic to Jesus. It is seen in the freshness and zeal of Levi. The old bottles picture the stodginess and cold formalism of the Pharisees.

The final parable says no man having drunk old wine prefers new. In his view, the old is good enough. This pictures the natural reluctance of men to abandon the old for the new, Judaism for Christianity, law for grace, shadows for substance! "A man accustomed to forms, human arrangements, father's religion, etc., never likes the new principle and power of the kingdom" (J. N. Darby).

Disputes Over the Sabbath (6:1-11)

Two incidents concerning the Sabbath are now brought before us to show the mounting opposition of the religious leaders was reaching a climax.

On the first Sabbath, the Lord and His disciples walked through some grain fields. The disciples plucked some grains, rubbed them in their hands, and ate them. The Pharisees could not quarrel about the fact of the grain being taken; this was permitted by the law (Deut. 23:25). Their criticism was that it was done on the Sabbath. They called the plucking of grain a harvesting operation, and the rubbing of the grain a threshing operation.

The Lord answered using an incident from the life of David. The law of the Sabbath was never intended to forbid a work of necessity. Rejected and pursued, David and his men were hungry. They went into the house of God and ate the showbread, which was usually reserved for the priests. God made an exception in David's case. There was sin in Israel. The king was disallowed. The law concerning the showbread was never intended to be so slavishly followed as to permit God's king to starve.

Here was a similar situation. Christ and His disciples were hungry. The Pharisees would rather see them starve than pick wheat on the Sabbath. But Christ is Lord of the Sabbath. He gave the law in the first place; no one was better qualified than He to interpret its true spiritual meaning or to save it from misunderstanding.

The second incident involving the Sabbath concerned a miraculous cure. The scribes and Pharisees watched Jesus intently and maliciously to see if He would heal the man with a withered hand on the Sabbath. From past experience and their knowledge of Him, they had good reason to believe He would. The Lord did not disappoint them. He first asked the man to stand up in the middle of the crowd in the synagogue. This dramatic action drew the attention of all on what was about to happen.

Jesus asked His critics if it was right to do good on the Sabbath, or to do harm. If they answered correctly, they would have to say that it was right to do good on the Sabbath, and wrong to do harm. If it was right to do good, then He was doing good by healing the man. If it was wrong to do harm on the Sabbath, then they were breaking the Sabbath by plotting to kill the Lord Jesus.

There was no answer from the adversaries. Jesus then directed the man to stretch out his withered right hand. (Only Luke mentions it was the right hand.) With the command went the necessary power. As the man obeyed, his hand was made normal. The Pharisees and scribes were furious. They wanted to condemn Jesus for breaking the Sabbath. All He had done was speak a few words and the man was healed. No servile work was involved. Yet they plotted together how they might "get" Him.

The Sabbath was intended by God for man's good. When rightly understood, it did not prohibit a work of necessity or a work of mercy.

Jesus Calls the Twelve Disciples (6:12-19)

Jesus spent all night in prayer before choosing the twelve. What a rebuke this is to our impulsiveness and independence of God! Luke alone mentions this night of prayer. The twelve whom He chose from among the wider circle of disciples were:

1. *Simon Peter,* son of Jonas, and one of the most prominent of the apostles.

2. *Andrew,* brother of Peter. It was Andrew who introduced Peter to the Lord.

3. *James, the son of Zebedee.* He was privileged to go with Peter and John to the Mount of Transfiguration. He was killed by Herod Agrippa I.

4. *John,* the son of Zebedee. Jesus called James and John "Sons of Thunder." It was this John who wrote the gospel and the epistles bearing his name, and the book of Revelation.

5. *Philip,* a native of Bethsaida, who introduced Nathanael to Jesus. Not to be confused with Philip, the evangelist, in the book of Acts.

6. *Bartholomew,* generally understood to be another name for Nathanael, is mentioned only in the listings of the twelve.

7. *Matthew,* the tax-collector, was also named Levi. He is generally believed to have written the first gospel.

8. *Thomas,* also called Didymus, meaning twin. He said he would not believe the Lord had risen until he saw conclusive evidence.

9. *James, the son of Alphaeus.* He may have been the one who held a place of responsibility in the church at Jerusalem after James, the son of Zebedee, had been killed by Herod.

10. *Simon, the Zealot.* Little is known of him, as far as the sacred record is concerned.

11. *Judas,* the son (ASV) or brother (KJV) of James. Probably the same as Jude, the author of the epistle, and commonly believed to be Lebbaeus, whose surname was Thaddaeus (Matt. 10:3; Mark 3:18).

12. *Judas Iscariot*, presumed to be from Kerioth in Judah, and thus the only one of the apostles who was not from Galilee. The betrayer of our Lord, he was called by Jesus "the son of perdition."

The disciples were not necessarily men of outstanding intellects or abilities. They represented a cross-section of humanity. The thing that made them great was their relationship to Jesus and commitment to Him. They were probably young men in their twenties when the Savior chose them.

Jesus selected only twelve disciples. He was more interested in quality than quantity. Given the right caliber of men, He could send them out and by spiritual reproduction could evangelize the world. Once the disciples were chosen, it was important that they should be thoroughly trained in the principles of the kingdom of God. The rest of the chapter is devoted to a summary of the type of character and behavior the disciples of the Lord Jesus are to have.

Notice the following discourse is not the same as the Sermon on the Mount (Matthew 5-7). It was delivered on a mountain; this was delivered on a plain, or level space (v. 17). It also had blessings but no woes; this has both. There are other differences—in words, length, and emphasis.

Notice too this message of stern discipleship was given to the multitude as well as to the twelve. It seems whenever a great multitude followed Jesus, He tested their sincerity by speaking quite bluntly to them. People had come from Judea and Jerusalem in the south, from Tyre and Sidon in the west, Gentiles as well as Jews. Diseased people and demoniacs pressed close to touch Jesus; they knew that healing power flowed out from Him.

Blessings and Woes (6:20-26)

It is very important to realize how revolutionary Christ's teachings are. Remember, He was going to the cross. He would die, be buried, rise the third day and return to heaven. The good news of free salvation must go out to the world. The redemption of men depended on their hearing the message. How could the world be evangelized?

Astute leaders of this world would organize a vast army, provide liberal finances, generous food supplies, entertainment for the morale of the men, and good public relations. Jesus chose twelve disciples and sent them out poor, hungry, weeping, and persecuted. Can the world be evangelized that way? Yes, and in no other way!

The Savior began with four blessings and four woes. "Blessed be you poor." Not blessed are *the* poor but blessed be *you* (plural) poor. Poverty in itself is not a blessing; it is more often a curse. Here Jesus was speaking about a self-imposed poverty for His sake. He was not speaking of people who are poor because of laziness, tragedy, or reasons beyond their control. He was referring to those who purposely choose to be poor in order to share their Savior with others.

When you think of it, it is the only sensible, reasonable approach. Suppose the disciples had gone forth as wealthy men. People would have flocked to the banner of Christ with the hope of becoming rich. As it was, the disciples could not promise them silver and gold. If they came at all, it would only be in quest of spiritual blessing. Also if the disciples had been rich, they would have missed the blessing of constant dependence on the Lord, and of proving His faithfulness. *George Müller*

The kingdom of God belongs to those who are satisfied with the supply of their current needs so everything above can go into the work of the Lord.

"Blessed are you who hunger now." Once again this does not mean the vast hordes of humanity who are suffering from malnutrition. Instead it refers to disciples of Jesus Christ who deliberately adopt a life of self-denial in order to help alleviate human need, both spiritual and physical. It is people who are willing to get along on a plain, inexpensive diet rather than deprive others of the gospel by their indulgence. All such self-denial will be rewarded in a future day.

"Blessed are you who weep now." Sorrow in itself is not a blessing; the weeping of unsaved people has no lasting benefit connected with it. Here Jesus is speaking about tears that are shed for His sake. Tears for lost, perishing mankind; tears over the divided, impotent state of the church. All sorrow endured in serving the Lord Christ. Those who sow in tears will reap in joy.

"Blessed are you when men hate you . . . exclude you . . . revile you . . . cast out your name as evil." This blessing is not for those who suffer for their own sins or folly. It is for those who are despised, excommunicated, reproached, and slandered because of their loyalty to Christ.

The key to understanding these four beatitudes is found in the phrase "for the Son of Man's sake." Things that in themselves would be a curse become a blessing when willingly endured for Him. But the motive must be love for Christ, otherwise, the most heroic sacrifices are worthless. Persecution for Christ is cause for great rejoicing because it will bring a great reward in heaven, and it associates the sufferer with His faithful witness of past ages.

The four blessings describe the ideal man in the kingdom of God as the one who lives sacrificially, soberly, and enduringly. The four woes present by contrast those who are least esteemed in Christ's new society, the very ones who are counted great in the world today.

"Woe to you who are rich." There are serious moral problems connected with the hoarding of wealth in a world where several thousand die daily of starvation and millions are deprived of the good news of salvation through faith in Christ. These words of the Lord Jesus should be pondered carefully by Christians who are tempted to lay up treasures on earth, to hoard, and to save for a rainy day. To do this is to live for the wrong world.

Incidentally, this woe on the rich shows that when the Lord said "Blessed are you poor . . ." in verse 20, He did not mean poor in spirit. Otherwise verse 24 would have to mean "woe to you that are rich in spirit," and such a meaning is out of the question. The

> To lay up treasures on earth is to live for the wrong world.

meaning of verse 24 is simply that those who have wealth and who fail to use it for the eternal enrichment of others have already received the only reward they will ever get—the selfish, here-and-now gratification of their desires.

"Woe to you who are full." These are believers who think only the best of this world is good enough. The Lord says they will hunger in a coming day when rewards are given out for faithful, sacrificial discipleship.

"Woe to you who laugh now." This woe is aimed at those whose lives are a continuous cycle of amusement, entertainment, and pleasure, acting as if life were made for fun, and seem oblivious of the desperate condition of men outside of Jesus Christ. Those who laugh now will mourn and weep when they look back over wasted opportunities, selfish indulgence, and their own spiritual impoverishment.

"Woe to you when all men speak well of you." Why? Because it is a sure sign you are not living the life or faithfully proclaiming the message.

It is in the very nature of a righteous life to convict the unrighteous. It is the very nature of the gospel to offend the ungodly.

Those who receive their applause from the world are fellow-travelers with the false prophets of the Old Testament who tickled the people's ears with what they wanted to hear. They were more interested in the favor of men than in the praise of God.

The Secret Weapon (6:27-38)

Now the Lord Jesus unveils to His disciples a secret weapon from the arsenal of God: the weapon of love. This will be one of their most effective weapons in evangelizing the world.

When Jesus speaks of love, He is not referring to the human emotion. This is supernatural love. Only those who are born again can know it or display it. It is utterly impossible for anyone who does not have the indwelling Holy Spirit.

A murderer may love his own children, but that is not love as Jesus intended. The one is human affection; the other is divine love. The first requires only physical life; the second requires divine life. The first is largely a matter of the emotions; the second is largely a matter of the will. Anyone can love his friends, but it takes supernatural power to love his enemies. And *that* is the love (Greek—*agape*) of the New Testament. It means to do good to those who hate you, to bless those who curse you, to pray for those who treat you meanly, and ever and always to turn the other cheek.

"In its deepest sense love is the prerequisite of Christianity. To feel toward enemies what others feel toward friends; to descend as rain and sunbeams on the unjust as well as the just; to minister to those who are unprepossessing and repellent as others minister to the attractive and winsome; to be always the same, not subject to moods or fancies or whims; to suffer long; to take no account of evil; to rejoice with the truth; to bear, believe, hope, and endure all things, never to fail—this is love, and such love is the achievement of the Holy Spirit. We cannot achieve it ourselves."[1]

> The world does not know how to deal with someone who repays every wrong with kindness.

This love is unbeatable. The world can usually conquer the man who fights back; it is used to jungle warfare and to the principle of retaliation;

but it does not know how to deal with someone who repays every wrong with kindness. It is utterly confused and disorganized by such other-worldly behavior. When robbed of its overcoat, love offers its suit-coat as well, never turns away from any genuine case of need. When unjustly deprived of property, it does not ask for reimbursement.

Unsaved men can love those who love them. This does not require divine life nor does it make any impact upon the world of unsaved men. Jesus repeated (v. 35) that we should love our enemies, do good, and lend, hoping for nothing in return. Such behavior is distinctly Christian and marks those who are the sons of the Highest. Men become sons of the Most High only by receiving Jesus Christ as Lord and Savior (John 1:12). This is the way true believers *manifest* themselves to the world as sons of God.

God treated us in the way described in verses 27-35. He is kind to the unthankful and the evil. When we act like Him, we manifest the family likeness, showing we have been born of God. To be merciful means to forgive when it is in our power to avenge. God showed mercy by not giving us the punishment we deserved. He wants us to show mercy to others.

> **To be merciful means to forgive when it is in our power to avenge.**

There are two things love doesn't do—judge or condemn. Jesus said, "Judge not, and you shall not be judged." First, we must not judge people's motives; as we cannot read the heart, we cannot know why a person acts as he does. Nor are we to judge another Christian's stewardship or service (1 Cor. 4:1–5); God is the Judge. We must not be censorious; a critical, faultfinding spirit violates the law of love.

But there are certain areas where a Christian must judge. He must often judge whether other people are true Christians to recognize an unequal yoke (2 Cor. 6:14). Sin must be judged in the home and the assembly. We must judge between good and evil, but must not impugn motives or assassinate character.

> **There are areas where a Christian must judge.**

"Forgive, and you will be forgiven." This makes our forgiveness dependent on our willingness to forgive. But other Scriptures teach when we receive Christ by faith, we are freely and unconditionally forgiven. How can we reconcile this seeming contradiction? We are speaking of two different types of forgiveness: judicial and parental. *Judicial forgiveness* is what is granted by God the Judge to everyone who believes on the Lord Jesus Christ. He has met the penalty of sins and the believing sinner will not have to pay it. It is unconditional. *Parental forgiveness* is what God the Father grants to His erring child when he confesses and forsakes his sin. It results in the restoration of fellowship in the family of God, and has nothing to do with the penalty of sin. As Father, God cannot forgive us when we are unwilling to forgive one another. He cannot walk in fellowship with those who do. It is parental forgiveness that Jesus refers to in the words ". . . and you will be forgiven."

—————— ❧ ——————
Those who give generously are rewarded generously.
—————— ❧ ——————

Love is manifested in giving (see John 3:16; Eph. 5:25). The Christian ministry is expenditure. Those who give generously are rewarded generously. The picture in verse 38 is of a man with a large apron-like fold in the front of his garment. He uses it for carrying seed. The more widely he broadcasts the seed, the greater his harvest. He is rewarded with good measure, pressed down, shaken together, and running over. He receives it into the bosom of his garment. A fixed principle in life is we reap according to our sowing, our actions react upon us, what we measure out to others is measured back to us again.

Parable of the Blind Hypocrites (6:39-45)

In the previous section the Lord Jesus taught that the disciples were to have a ministry of giving. Now He says the extent to which they can be a blessing to others is limited by their own spiritual condition. If we are blind to certain truths of God's Word, we cannot help someone else in those areas. If there are blind-spots in our spiritual life, we can be sure that there will be blind-spots in the lives of our understudies.

"A disciple is not above his teacher, but everyone who is perfectly trained will be like his teacher" (v. 40). The more he teaches them, the more they become like him. But his own stage of growth forms the upper limit to which he can bring them.

The important truth is still more strikingly brought out in the illustration of the mote and the beam. One day a man is walking past a threshing floor where the grain is being beaten out. A sudden gust of wind lifts a tiny particle of chaff and lands it squarely in his eye. He rubs the eye to get rid of the irritant, but the more he rubs it, the more irritated it becomes. Just then another man comes along, sees the distress of the first, and offers to help. But this man has a telephone pole sticking out of his own eye. He can scarcely help because he cannot see what he is doing. The obvious lesson is that a teacher cannot speak to his disciples about blemishes in their lives if he has the same blemishes to an exaggerated degree in his own life and cannot see them. If we are to be a help to others, our own lives must be exemplary. Otherwise they will say to us, "Physician, heal yourself!"

The fourth illustration the Lord uses is the tree and its fruit. A good tree brings forth fruit, good or bad, depending on what it is in itself. We judge a tree by the kind and quality of fruit it bears. So it is in the area of discipleship. A man who is morally pure and spiritually healthy can bring forth blessing for others out of the good treasure of his heart. On the other hand, a man who is basically impure can bring forth only evil.

In verses 39-45 the Lord is telling the disciples that their ministry is to be a ministry of character. What they are is more important than anything they will ever say or do. The final result of their service will be determined by what they are in themselves.

Obedience Is What Counts (6:46-49)

"Why do you call me 'Lord, Lord,' and not do the things which I say?" The word *Lord* means Master, meaning He has complete authority over our lives, we belong to Him, and are obligated to do whatever He says. To call Him "Lord" and fail to obey Him is absurdly contradictory. A mere professed acknowledgment of His lordship is not enough. True love and faith involve obedience. We don't really love Him or really believe Him if we don't do what He says. As Geoffrey O'Hara says:

> Ye call me the "Way" and walk me not,
> Ye call me the "Life" and live me not,
> Ye call me "Master" and obey me not,
> If I condemn thee, blame me not.

> Ye call me "Bread" and eat me not,
> Ye call me "Truth" and believe me not,
> Ye call me "Lord" and serve me not,
> If I condemn thee, blame me not.

To further enforce this important truth, the Lord Jesus gives the story of the two builders. Commonly this story is applied to the gospel by saying the wise man is descriptive of the one who believes and is saved and the foolish man is the one who rejects Christ and is lost. This is a valid application. But if we interpret the story in its context, we find a deeper meaning.

The wise man comes to Christ (salvation), hears His words (instruction), and does them (obedience). He builds his life on such principles of Christian discipleship as are laid down in this chapter. This is the right way to build a life. When the house is battered by floods and streams, it stands firm because it has true spiritual stability.

The foolish man hears (instruction) but fails to follow the teaching (disobedience). He builds his life on what he thinks best, following the carnal principles of this world. When the storms of life rage, his house has no foundation and is swept away. His soul may be saved but his life is lost.

The wise man is poor and hungry, mourns, and is persecuted—all for the Son of Man's sake. The world would call such a man foolish. Jesus calls him wise. The foolish man is rich, feasts luxuriously, lives for fun, and is popular with everyone. The world calls him a wise man. Jesus calls him foolish.

---

[1] F. B. Meyer, *The Heavenlies* (Westchester, Illinois: Good News Publishers, n.d.) p. 26.

4

MIRACLES AND PARABLES
(7:1–8:56)

Jesus Heals the Centurion's Servant (7:1-10)

At the conclusion of His discourse, Jesus left the multitude and went into the city of Capernaum. There some elders of the Jews came to ask help for the servant of a Gentile centurion. It seems that this centurion was especially kind to the Jewish people, even going so far as to build a synagogue for them. Like all the centurions in the New Testament, he is presented in a good light (Luke 23:47; Acts 10:1-48).

It was unusual for a master to be so kind toward a bondservant as he was. When the servant took sick, the centurion asked the elders of the Jews to beg Jesus to heal him. This Roman officer is the only one who sought blessing from Jesus for a servant, as far as we know.

It was a strange position for the elders to be in. They did not believe in Jesus, yet their friendship for the centurion forced them to go to Jesus in a time of need. They said concerning the centurion, "He is deserving [worthy]" (v. 4). But when the centurion met Jesus, he said, "I am not worthy" (v. 6); he used a different word for worthy meaning "I am not important enough."

According to Matthew's gospel, the centurion went directly to Jesus. Here in Luke, he sent the elders. Both are correct. First, he sent the elders, and then went out himself to Jesus. The humility and faith of the centurion are remarkable. He did not consider himself worthy that Jesus should enter his house. Neither did he consider himself worthy to come to Jesus in person. But he had faith to believe that Jesus could heal without being bodily present. A word from Him would drive out the sickness.

The centurion went on to explain that he knew something about authority and responsibility, having considerable experience in this area. He himself was under the authority of the Roman government and was responsible to carry out its orders. In addition, he had soldiers under him who were instantly obedient to his orders. He recognized Jesus' authority over diseases was the same as the Roman government had over him, and he had over his subordinates.

No wonder Jesus marveled at the faith of this Gentile centurion. No one in Israel had made such a bold confession of Jesus' absolute authority. Such faith could never go unrewarded. When the centurion and elders returned to the house, they found the servant was completely recovered. This is one of two times in the gospels when we read that Jesus marveled: He marveled at the faith of this Gentile centurion and the unbelief of Israel (Mark 6:6).

Jesus Raises the Widow's Son to Life (7:11-17)

Nain was a hamlet southwest of Capernaum. As Jesus approached, He saw a funeral procession for the only son of a widow leaving the city. The Lord had compassion on the bereft mother. Touching the frame on which the body was carried (apparently to stop the procession) Jesus ordered the young man to arise. Immediately life returned to the corpse, and the lad sat up. Thus the Lord had power over death, as well as over disease, and He restored the boy to his mother.

Consternation seized the people. They had witnessed a mighty miracle. The dead had been raised to life. They believed the Lord Jesus was a great prophet sent by God. But when they said "God has visited His people," they did not necessarily mean Jesus Himself was God. They felt the miracle was evidence that God was working in their midst in an impersonal way. Their report of the miracle spread throughout all the surrounding area.

Dr. Luke's casebook records Jesus' restoration of three "only children": the widow's son; Jairus's daughter (8:42); and the child possessed by demons (9:38).

John the Baptist Reassured (7:18-23)

News of Jesus' miracles filtered back to John the Baptist in prison at the castle of Machuerus, on the eastern shore of the Dead Sea. John sent two of his disciples to ask Jesus if He were really the Messiah, or if the Messiah was still to come!

―――――― ❧ ――――――
The best of men suffer brief lapses of faith.
―――――― ❧ ――――――

It may seem strange to us that John should ever question Jesus' messiahship. But we must remember the best of men suffer brief lapses of faith; physical distress can lead to severe mental depression. Jesus answered John's question by reminding him of the miracles He was doing and Isaiah had predicted would be performed by the Messiah (Isa. 35:5, 6; 61:1). Then He added a postscript to John, "Blessed is he who is not offended because of me." This may be understood as a rebuke; John had been offended by the failure of Jesus to seize the reins of authority and to manifest Himself in the way people expected. It may also be an exhortation to John not to abandon his faith.

Jesus Praises His Forerunner (7:24-35)

Jesus had nothing but praise for John. When the people had flocked out to the desert near Jordan, what had they expected to find? A fickle, spineless, wavering opportunist? No one could ever accuse John of being a reed shaken by the wind. Had they then expected to find a playboy, fashionably dressed and living in luxury and ease? That is the type of person who hangs around kings' palaces, seeking to enjoy all the pleasures of the court and to make endless contacts for his own profit and gratification. It was a prophet they went out to see—an embodied conscience who declared the word of the living God no matter what the cost might be. Indeed, he was more than a prophet. He himself was the subject of prophecy, and had the unique privilege of introducing the King.

Jesus quoted Malachi 3:1, showing a messenger had been promised in the Old Testament. He made a very interesting change in the pronouns. In Malachi 3:1, we read, "Behold, I send My messenger, and he will prepare the way before *Me*." But Jesus quoted it, "Behold, I send My messenger before *your* face, who will prepare *Your* way before *You*." The pronoun *Me* is changed to *You*. Godet explains this change as follows: "In the prophet's view, He who was sending, and He before whom the way was to be prepared, were one and the same person, Jehovah—hence the *before Me* in Malachi. But for Jesus, who, in speaking of Himself, never confounds Himself with the Father, a distinction became necessary. It is not Jehovah who speaks of

Himself, but Jehovah speaking to Jesus; hence the form *before You*. From which evidence, does it not follow from this quotation that, in the prophet's idea, as well as in that of Jesus, Messiah's appearing is the appearing of Jehovah?"[1]

Among those born of women, there was not a greater prophet than John, Jesus said. This superiority referred not to his personal character but to his position as forerunner of the Messiah. There were other men who matched him in zeal and honor and devotion. But no one else had the privilege of announcing the coming of the King. This made John unique. Yet, the Lord added, the least one in the kingdom of God is greater than John. To enjoy the blessings of the kingdom is greater than to be the forerunner of the King.

Jesus is recalling the reception given to John's preaching (v. 29). The common people and avowed sinners, like tax-collectors, repented and were baptized in the Jordan. In believing John's message and acting upon it, the people reckoned God to be righteous in demanding that the people of Israel should first repent before Christ could reign over them. They "justified God" means to account God as being right in His decrees and requirements.

The Pharisees and teachers of the law rejected God's program for their welfare by refusing to submit to John's baptism. It was impossible to please the generation of which they were the leaders. Jesus likened them to children playing in the street, not wanting to play either wedding or funeral. They were perverse, wayward, unpredictable, and hard-to-please. John the Baptist gave them an example of austerity, asceticism, and self-denial. They didn't like it, but criticized him as demon-possessed. Jesus identified Himself with those whom He came to bless by eating and drinking with tax-collectors and sinners. The Pharisees were unhappy, calling Him a glutton and a drinker. Fast or feast, funeral or wedding, John or Jesus—nothing and no one pleased them.

"We must give up the idea of trying to please everyone. The thing is impossible, and the attempt is mere waste of time. We must be content to walk in Christ's steps, and let the world say what it likes. Do what we will, we shall never satisfy it, or silence its ill-natured remarks. It first found fault with John the Baptist and then with his blessed Master. And it will go on finding fault with that Master's disciples so long as one of them is left upon earth."[2]

"But wisdom is justified by all her children" (v. 35). Wisdom here represents the Savior Himself. The small minority of disciples who honor

Him are wisdom's children. Even though the mass of the people reject Him, His true followers will vindicate His claims by lives of love, holiness, and devotedness.

Visit of Jesus to Simon's House (7:36-50)

In the following incident we have a sinful woman illustrating wisdom being justified by one of her children. As Dr. H. C. Woodring said so pointedly, "When God cannot get religious leaders to appreciate Christ, He will get harlots to do so."

Simon, the Pharisee, had invited Jesus to his house for a meal. A sinful woman appeared in the room at the same time. This unnamed woman brought a white translucent vital of perfume. Jesus was reclining on a couch while eating, with His head near the table. She stood at His feet, washing them with her tears, wiping them with her hair, and kissing them repeatedly. Then she anointed Him with the costly perfume. Such worship and sacrifice revealed her conviction that there was nothing too good for Jesus.

Simon's attitude was quite different. He felt that prophets, like Pharisees, should be separate from sinners. If Jesus were truly a prophet, he concluded, He would not let this woman bestow such affection on Him.

Jesus told the story of the moneylender and the two debtors. One owed fifty dollars, the other five (J.B. Phillips' paraphrase). When neither of them could repay at all, he cancelled both debts. At this point Jesus asked Simon which borrower would love the lender most. The Pharisee correctly answered, "The one whom he forgave more." In admitting this, he condemned himself, as Jesus proceeded to show him.

From the time the Lord had entered the house, the woman had lavished affection upon Him. The Pharisee, by contrast, had given Him a very cool reception, not even attending to the usual courtesies, such as washing the guest's feet, kissing His cheek,

We are all sinners. We can all know forgiveness.

and giving Him oil for His head. The woman had the consciousness of having been forgiven much. But Simon did not feel he had been a great sinner at all. ". . . to whom little is forgiven, the same loves little."

Jesus did not suggest the Pharisee was not a great sinner. He emphasized that Simon had never truly acknowledged his vast guilt and been forgiven.

If he had, he would have loved the Lord as deeply as the woman. We are all great sinners. We can all know great forgiveness. We can all love the Lord greatly.

Jesus took this occasion to announce publicly the forgiveness of this woman's sins. She had not been forgiven because of her love to Christ, but her love was a result of her forgiveness. She loved much because she had been forgiven much. The other guests inwardly questioned Jesus' right to forgive sins. But Jesus again assured the woman that her faith had saved her and she should go in peace.

Our Lord's conduct in eating at this Pharisee's table is quoted by some Christians in defense of the practice of keeping up intimacy with unconverted people, going to their amusements, and indulging in their pleasures. "Those who use such an argument would do well to remember our Lord's behavior on this occasion. He carried His 'Father's business' with Him to the Pharisee's table. He testified against the Pharisee's besetting sin. He explained to the Pharisee the nature of free forgiveness of sins, and the secret of true love to Himself. He declared the saving nature of faith. If Christians who argue in favor of intimacy with unconverted people will visit their houses in the spirit of our Lord, and speak and behave as He did, let them by all means continue the practice. But do they speak and behave at the tables of their unconverted acquaintances as Jesus did at Simon's table? This is a question they would do well to answer."[3]

Jesus' Ministry Continues in Galilee (8:1-3)

It is good to remember that the Gospels contain only a few incidents from the life and ministry of our Lord. The Holy Spirit selected those subjects that are included, but passed over many others. Here we have a simple, summary statement that Jesus ministered with His disciples in the cities and villages of Galilee. As He preached and announced the good news of the Kingdom of God, He was ministered to, probably in the way of food and lodging, by women who had been blessed by Him. For instance, there was Mary Magdalene who had been wonderfully delivered from seven demons. Some think she was a titled lady from Magdala (Migdol). There was Joanna, the wife of Herod's steward. Susanna was another, and there were more. Their kindness to our Lord did not go unnoticed or unrecorded. Little did they think as they shared their possessions with Jesus that Christians of all subsequent ages would read of their generosity and hospitality.

The subject of the Lord's ministry was the good news of the kingdom of God. The kingdom of God means the realm, visible or invisible, where God's rule is acknowledged. Matthew's use of "the kingdom of heaven" is basically the same; it simply means that "the Most High rules in the kingdom of men" (Dan. 4:17) or that "Heaven rules" (Dan. 4:26).

There are various stages of development of the kingdom in the New Testament. First of all, the kingdom was announced by John the Baptist as being "at hand" (Matt. 3:1-2). Then the kingdom was actually present in the Person of the King ("the kingdom of God is in the midst of you," Luke 17:21, Darby). This was the good news of the kingdom that Jesus announced. He offered Himself as Israel's King (Luke 23:3). Next we see the kingdom rejected by the nation of Israel (Luke 19:14; John 19:15). Today the kingdom is in mystery form (Matt. 13:11). Christ, the King, is temporarily absent, but His rule is acknowledged in the hearts of some people on earth. In one sense the kingdom today embraces all who even profess to accept the rule of God, even if they are not truly converted. This sphere of outward profession is seen in the parable of the sower and the seed (Luke 8:4-15), the wheat and the tares (Matt. 13:24-30) and the fish in the dragnet (Matt. 13:47-50). But in its deeper, truer sense, the kingdom includes only those who have been converted (Matt. 18:3) or born again (John 3:3). This is the sphere of inward reality.

The kingdom will one day be set up in a literal sense here on earth and the Lord Jesus will reign for one thousand years as King of kings and Lord of lords (Rev. 11:15; 19:16; 20:4). The final phase is known as the everlasting kingdom of our Lord and Savior Jesus Christ (2 Peter 1:11). This is the kingdom in eternity.

The Parable of the Sower (8:4-15)

The parable of the sower describes the kingdom in its present aspect. It teaches us that the kingdom of God includes profession as well as reality, forming the basis for a very solemn warning as to how we hear the word of God. Those who hear are more responsible than they ever were before. If they shrug off the message, or consider obedience an optional matter, they do so to their own loss. But if they hear and obey, they put themselves in a position to receive more light from God. The parable was spoken to a multitude, and then explained to the disciples.

The parable told of a sower, the seed, four kinds of soil where the seed was received, and four results. The wayside soil was trampled by men and devoured by birds. In the rocky soil the seed withered away for lack of moisture. In the thorny soil growth was choked by thorns. In the good ground the seed brought forth one hundred grains for each seed.

The Lord ended the parable with the words, "He who has ears to hear, let him hear!" In other words, when you hear the word of God, be careful what kind of reception you give to it. The seed must fall into good ground in order to become fruitful.

———— ✑ ————

When you hear the word of God, be careful what kind of reception you give to it.

———— ✑ ————

When the disciples inquired concerning the parable's meaning, the Lord Jesus explained that the mysteries of the kingdom of God would not be understood by everyone. Because the disciples were willing to trust and obey, they would be given the ability to understand the teachings of Christ. But Jesus purposely presented many truths in the form of parables so those who had no real love for Him would not understand; so that seeing, they might not see, and hearing they might not hear. In one sense, they saw and heard. They knew Jesus had talked about a sower and his seed. But they did not understand the deeper meaning of the illustration. They did not realize the hardness of their hearts.

Only to the disciples did the Lord explain the parable. Because they had already accepted the teaching they would be given more. Jesus explained the seed, God's message, was His own teaching. The wayside hearers heard the word only in a superficial way, where it remained on the surface of their lives. This made it easy for the devil (the birds of the heaven) to snatch it away. The rock-hearers heard the word too, but they did not let it break them; they remained unrepentant. No encouragement (moisture) was given to the seed, so it withered away and died. Perhaps they made a bright profession of faith at first, but there was no reality. There seemed to be life, but there was no root beneath the surface. When trouble came, their Christian profession was abandoned. The thorny ground hearers seemed to get along nicely for a while, but proved they were not genuine believers by their failure to go on steadfastly. The cares, riches, and pleasures of life took control, and the word was stifled and smothered. The good ground represented true believers whose hearts were honest and good. They not only received the word but allowed it to mold their lives. They were teachable and obedient. They developed true Christian characters and produced fruit for God.

J. N. Darby has well summarized this section: "If, on hearing, I possess that which I hear, not merely have joy in receiving it, but possess it as my own, then it becomes a part of the substance of my soul, and I shall get more; for when the truth has become a substance in my soul, there is a capacity for receiving more."

Man's Responsibility in Sharing Christ's Words (8:16-21)

At first glance there seems little connection between this section and the previous one. There is, however, a continuous flow of thought. The Savior is still emphasizing the importance of what His disciples do with His teachings. He likens Himself to a man who has lit a lamp, putting it on a lampstand for all to see the light, and not under a vessel or bed. In teaching the disciples the principles of the kingdom of God, He was lighting a lamp. What should they do with it?

First, they should not hide it under a vessel. In Matthew 5:15, Mark 4:21 and Luke 11:33, the vessel is spoken of as a bushel (a unit of measure used in the world of commerce). Hiding the lamp under a bushel speaks of allowing one's testimony to be obscured or crowded out in the rush of business life. It would be better to put the lamp on top of the bushel by practicing Christianity in the market place and using one's business as a pulpit for propagating the gospel. Second, the lamp should not be hid under a bed. The bed speaks of rest, comfort, laziness, and indulgence. How these can hinder the light from shining! By putting the lamp on a stand the disciple would live and preach the truth so everyone can see.

Verse 17 suggests that if we allow the message to be confined because of business or laziness, our neglect and failure will be

> If we are faithful in sharing the truth with others, God will reveal new and deeper truths to us.

exposed. Hiding the truth will be made manifest, and keeping it a secret will be brought to light. Therefore we should be careful *how* we hear. If we are faithful in sharing the truth with others, God will reveal new and deeper truths to us. If we do not have the spirit of evangelistic zeal, God will deprive us of the truth we think we possess. What we don't use, we lose.

VIP

"The disciples listened with a mind eager to understand and ready to believe and to obey: the rest heard with either listlessness, or curiosity, or resolute opposition. To the former more knowledge would be granted: the latter would be deprived of what knowledge they seemed to have."[14]

8:19 At this point in His discourse, Jesus was told that His mother and His brothers were waiting to see Him. Because of the crowd, they could not get near Him. The Lord's answer was that real relationship with Him depends on obedience to what God is saying, not natural ties. The ones He recognizes as members of His family are all who tremble at the word, who receive it with meekness, and who obey it implicitly. No crowd can prevent His spiritual family from having audience with Him.

Christ Stills the Tempest (8:22-25)

In the remainder of this chapter, Jesus is seen exercising His lordship over the elements, demons, disease, and death. All these obey His word; only man refuses. Violent storms rise quickly on the Sea of Galilee, making navigation perilous. Yet perhaps this particular storm was of satanic origin; it might have been an attempt to destroy the Savior of the world.

> **To be with Christ is to be absolutely safe and secure.**

Jesus was asleep when the storm broke. His sleeping is evidence of His true humanity. The storm went to sleep when Jesus spoke; this attests to His absolute deity. The disciples, expressing anguished fears for their own safety, awoke Jesus. With perfect poise, He rebuked the waves and wind; all was calm. What He did to the Sea of Galilee, He can do to the troubled, storm-tossed disciple. He asked the disciples, "Where is your faith?" They should not have worried. They need not have awakened Him. To be with Christ in the boat is to be absolutely safe and secure.

The disciples did not fully appreciate the extent of the Master's power. Their understanding of Him was defective. The elements obeying Him made them marvel. They were no different from us. In the storms of life, we often despair. Then when the Lord comes to our aid, we are astonished at the display of His power, wondering at the shallowness of our trust.

Jesus Heals Legion, the Demoniac (8:26-39)

When Jesus and His disciples reached shore, they were in the district of the Gerasenes, called Gadarenes. There they met a man possessed with demons. Matthew mentions two demoniacs, while Mark and Luke speak of only one. Such seeming discrepancies might indicate that they were actually two different occasions, or one writer gave a fuller account than the others.

This particular case of demon-possession caused the victim to discard his clothing, shun society, and live in tombs. When he saw Jesus, he begged Him to let him alone. Of course, it was the evil spirits who spoke through the pitiful man.

Demon-possession is real and not mere influences. These were supernatural beings that indwelt the man, controlling his thoughts, speech, and behavior. These particular demons caused the man to be extremely violent. When he had one of these violent convulsions, he broke the chains restraining him and ran off to the wilderness. This is not surprising when we realize there were enough demons cooped up within this one man to destroy about 2,000 pigs (see Mark 5:13).

The man's name was Legion. These demons recognized Jesus as the Son of the Most High God. They knew too their doom was inevitable and He would bring it to pass. But they were looking for a reprieve, begging Him not to command them to depart at once into the pit of hell. They sought permission to enter a herd of swine nearby on the mountain. This permission was granted, with the result that the pigs ran headlong down the slopes into the Sea of Galilee and drowned.

The Lord is criticized today for destroying the property of someone else. However, if the swine keepers were Jews they were engaged in an unclean business. And whether they were Jews or Gentiles, they should have valued one man more than a few thousand pigs.

The news quickly spread throughout the region. When a great crowd gathered, they saw the former demoniac completely restored to normal sanity and decency. The Gerasenes became so upset that they asked Jesus to leave. "The world beseeches Jesus to depart, desiring their own ease, which is more disturbed by the presence and power of God, than by a legion of devils. He goes away. The man who was healed desires to be with Him, but the Lord sends him back . . . to be a witness of the grace and power of which he had been the subject."[5]

Later, when Jesus visited Decapolis, a sympathetic crowd met Him (Mark 7:31-37). Could this have been the result of the faithful witness of the healed demoniac? *Psalm 46*

Jairus Pleads for Jesus' Help (8:40-42)

Jesus returned to the western shore of the Sea of Galilee. There another crowd was waiting for Him. Jairus, a ruler of the synagogue, was especially anxious to see Him because his twelve-year-old daughter was dying. He urgently begged Jesus to go with him quickly. But the multitude surged around Him, hindering His progress.

A Woman Interrupts and Is Healed (8:43-48)

In the crowd was a timid, yet desperate woman, who had been afflicted with a bloody drainage for twelve years. Luke, the physician, admits she had spent her life-savings and income on doctors without getting any help. Mark adds the unprofessional touch that she actually got worse.

She sensed there was power in Jesus to heal her, so she eased her way through the crowd to where He was and touched the hem of His garment (the border or fringe that formed the lower border of a Jew's coat, Num. 15:38-39; Deut. 22:12; Zech. 8:23). Immediately the blood stopped flowing and she was completely cured. Trying to steal away quietly, her escape was blocked by a question from Jesus, "Who touched Me?" Peter and the other disciples thought this was an inane question: all kinds of people were shoving, pushing, touching Him.

But Jesus recognized a touch that was different. As someone has said, "The flesh throngs, but faith touches." He knew faith had touched Him, because He sensed an outflow of power—the power to heal the woman. This did not mean He was any less powerful than He had been, but simply it cost Him something to heal. There was expenditure.

The woman came trembling before Him saying publicly why she had touched Him and what had happened. Her public confession was rewarded with a public commendation of her faith by Jesus, and a public pronouncement of His peace upon her.

No one ever touches Jesus by faith without His knowing it, and without receiving a blessing. No one ever confesses Him openly without being strengthened in assurance of salvation.

Jesus Restores the Daughter of Jairus (8:49-56)

The healing of the woman with the issue of blood probably did not delay Jesus very long, but long enough for a messenger to arrive with the news that Jairus's daughter had died—the Teacher's services, therefore, would no longer be needed. There was faith that He could heal, but none for His power to raise the dead. But Jesus would not be dismissed so easily. He answered with words of comfort, encouragement and promise. "Do not be afraid; only believe, and she will be made well."

As soon as He arrived at the home, He went to the room, taking only Peter, John, James, and the parents. Everyone was wailing in despair, but Jesus told them to stop because the girl was not dead, only sleeping. This caused them to ridicule Him, because they were positive she was dead.

Was she really dead, or was she in a deep sleep, like a coma? Most commentators say she was dead. They point out that Jesus referred to Lazarus as being asleep, meaning he was dead. Sir Robert Anderson says the girl was not really dead.[6] His arguments are as follows: (1) Jesus said the girl would "recover." The word He used for "recover" is the same word used in verse 48 of this chapter, where it refers to healing, not resurrection. The word is never used in the New Testament of raising the dead. (2) Jesus used a different word for sleeping in the case of Lazarus. (3) The people thought she was dead, but Jesus would not take credit for raising her from the dead when actually He knew she was only sleeping.

Anderson says it is simply a matter of whom you want to believe. Jesus said she was sleeping. The others thought they knew she was dead. In any case, Jesus said to her, "Little girl, arise." Immediately she arose. After restoring her to her parents, Jesus told them not to publicize the miracle. He was not interested in notoriety, in fickle public enthusiasm, in idle curiosity.

We have now come to the close of the second year of Jesus' public ministry. Chapter 9 opens the third year with the sending forth of the Twelve.

---

[1] F. L. Godet, Commentary on the Gospel of Luke, Vol. I (Grand Rapids: Zondervan Publishing House, n. d.) p. 350.

[2] John Charles Ryle, op. cit., p. 230.

[3] John Charles Ryle, op. cit., p. 239.

[4] G. H. Lang, The Parabolic Teaching of the Scripture (Grand Rapids: Wm. B. Eerdmans Publishing Company, 1956) p. 60.

[5] J. N. Darby, op. cit., p. 340.

[6] Sir Robert Anderson, Misunderstood Texts of the New Testament (London: Nisbet and Co., Ltd., 1916) p. 51.

5

TRAINING THE DISCIPLES
(9:1–10:42)

Jesus Sends Out the Twelve Disciples (9:1-6)

This incident closely resembles the sending of the twelve in Matthew 10:1-15, but with notable differences. In Matthew, the disciples were told to go only to the Jews, and to raise the dead, as well as heal the sick. There is no doubt a reason for the condensed version in Luke, but the reason is not obvious.

The Lord Jesus not only had power and authority to perform miracles, but He conferred this power and authority on others. *Power* means strength or ability; *authority* means the right to use it. The message of the disciples was confirmed by signs and wonders (Heb. 2:3-4) in the absence of the complete Bible in written form. This does not deny that God can heal miraculously today. Of course He can. But whether healing should still accompany the preaching of the gospel is certainly questionable.

> *Power* means strength or ability; *authority* means the right to use it.

Now the disciples would have an opportunity to practice the principles the Lord had taught them. They were to trust Him for the supply of their material needs—no food or money. They were to live very simply—no extra staff or extra coat. They were to stay in the first house where they were made welcome—no moving around in hopes of obtaining more comfortable lodging. They were not to prolong their stay or exert pressure on those who rejected the message, but were instructed to shake the dust from their feet as a testimony against them. It was presumably in the villages of Galilee that the disciples preached the gospel and healed the sick. Their message had to do with the kingdom, the announcement of the King's presence in their midst and His willingness to reign over a repentant people.

Herod's Perplexity (9:7-9)

Herod Antipas was tetrarch in Galilee and Perea at this time. He reigned over one-fourth of the territory originally included in the kingdom of his father, Herod the Great. Word reached him that someone was performing mighty miracles in his territory. Immediately his conscience began raising questions. The memory of John the Baptist still troubled him. Herod had silenced John's fearless voice by beheading him, but he was still haunted by the power of his life.

Some rumored that John had risen from the dead. Others guessed that it was Elijah or one of the other prophets. Herod tried quelling his anxiety by reminding others that he had beheaded John, but the fear remained. Who was this? He wished he could see Him but never did until just before Christ's crucifixion.

The power of a Spirit-filled life! The Lord Jesus, the obscure Carpenter of Nazareth, caused Herod to tremble without ever having met Him.

Jesus Feeds the Five Thousand (9:10-17)

When the disciples returned, they reported their results directly to the Lord Jesus. Our Lord then took them to a desert place adjoining Bethsaida (meaning *house of fishing*). It seems there were two Bethsaidas at this time, one on the west side of the sea of Galilee and this one on the east. The exact location is unknown.

Any hopes of a quiet time together were soon shattered. A crowd of people quickly gathered. The Lord Jesus was always accessible. He did not consider this an annoying interruption—in fact it specifically states "He received [welcomed] them," teaching them about the kingdom of God and healing those who needed it. As evening drew on, the disciples became restless. So many people needing food! An impossible situation. They asked the Lord to send the multitude away, but He would not. Let the disciples feed the crowd. They protested that they had only five loaves and two fish, forgetting they also had the unlimited resources of the Lord

Jesus to draw on. He simply asked the disciples to seat the crowd of 5,000 men, women, and children. After giving thanks, He broke the bread and gave it to the disciples. They distributed it to the people. There was plenty of food for everyone. When the meal was over there was more food left than there had been at the outset! The leftovers filled twelve baskets, one for each of the disciples.

This incident is filled with significance for disciples who are charged with the evangelization of the world. The 5,000 represent lost humanity, starving for the bread of God. The disciples picture helpless Christians, with seemingly limited resources, but unwilling to share what they have. The Lord's command "You give them something to eat" is simply a precursor of the great commission. The lesson is that if we give Jesus what we have, He can multiply it to feed the spiritually hungry multitude. The world could be evangelized in this generation if Christians would surrender to Christ all that they are and have. That is the enduring lesson of the feeding of the 5,000.

> ___ ✍ ___
> **If we give Jesus what we have, He can multiply it to feed the spiritually hungry multitude.**
> ___ ✍ ___

Discourse with the Disciples (9:18-22)

Immediately following the miraculous feeding of the multitude we have Peter's great confession of Christ at Caesarea Philippi. Did the miracle of the loaves and fish open the eyes of the disciples to see the glory of the Lord Jesus as God's Anointed One?

The incident at Caesarea Philippi is commonly acknowledged to be the watershed of the Savior's teaching ministry with the twelve. Up to this point He has been patiently leading them to an appreciation of who He is and what He could do in and through them. That goal has been reached; from this point on He moves on determinedly to the cross.

Verse 18 seems to be contradictory. It says Jesus was alone praying, but it also says His disciples were with Him. Although the disciples were with Jesus, He prayed alone. There is no record of the Lord Jesus ever praying with the disciples. He prayed for them in their presence and taught them to pray, but His own prayer life was separate from theirs.

Following one of His seasons of prayer, He questioned the disciples as to who men thought He was. They reported a difference of opinion—some said John the Baptist; others said Elijah; still others said one of the Old Testament prophets in resurrection. But when He asked the disciples, Peter confidently confessed Him as the Christ (or Messiah) of God.

Stewart's comments concerning this incident at Caesarea Philippi are excellent. "He began with the impersonal question: 'Who do the crowds say that I am?' That, at any rate, was not difficult to answer. For on every side, men were saying things about Jesus. A dozen verdicts were abroad. All kinds of rumors and opinions were in the air. Jesus was on every tongue. And men were not only saying things about Jesus; they were saying great things about Him, Some thought He was John the Baptist back from the dead. Others said He reminded them of Elijah. Others spoke of Jeremiah or another of the prophets. In other words, while current opinions were by no means unanimous as to Jesus' identity, they were unanimous that He was someone great. His place was among the heroes of His race.

"It is worth remarking that history here is repeating itself. Once again Jesus is on every tongue. He is being discussed today far beyond the circle of the Christian Church, And great is the diversity of verdicts about Him. Papini, looking at Jesus, sees the Poet. Bruce Barton sees the Man of Action. Middleton Murry sees the Mystic. Men with no brief for orthodoxy are ready to extol Jesus as the paragon of saints and captain of all moral leaders forever. 'Even now,' said John Stuart Mill, 'it would not be easy even for an unbeliever to find a better translation of the rule of virtue from the abstract into the concrete than to endeavor so to live that Christ would approve our life.' Like the men of His own day who called Him John, Elijah, Jeremiah, so the men of today are agreed that among the heroes and saints of all time Jesus stands supreme.

"But Jesus was not content with that recognition. People were saying that He was John, Elijah, Jeremiah. But that meant that He was one in a series. It meant that there were precedents and parallels, and that even if He stood first in rank, He was still only *primus inter peres,* first among His equals. But quite certainly that is not what the Christ of the New Testament claimed. Men may agree with Christ's claim, or they may dissent from it; but as to the fact of the claim itself there is not the shadow of a doubt. Christ claimed to be something and someone unprecedented, unparalleled, unrivaled, unique (for example Matthew 11:27; 10:37; 24:35; John 10:30; 14:6)."[1]

Following Peter's historic confession, Jesus instructed them not to tell others; nothing must interrupt His pathway to the cross. Then the Savior unveiled His own immediate future to them. He must suffer, must be rejected by the religious leaders of Israel, must be slain, and must be raised the third day. This was an astounding announcement. Let us not forget these words were spoken by the only sinless, righteous Man who ever lived on his earth. They were spoken by the true Messiah of Israel. They were the words of God manifest in the flesh.

They tell us that the life of fulfillment, the perfect life, the life of obedience to the will of God involves suffering, rejection, death in one form or another, and a resurrection to life that is deathless. It is a life poured out for others. This was the very opposite of the popular idea of Messiah's role. Men looked for an aggressive, enemy-destroying leader. It must have been a shock to the disciples. But if, as they confessed, Jesus was indeed the Christ of God, then they had no reason for disillusionment or discouragement. If He is the Anointed of God, then His cause can never fail. No matter what might happen to Him or to them, they were on the winning side. Victory and vindication were inevitable.

Invitation to Take Up the Cross (9:23-27)

———— ❧ ————

To take up the cross means to deliberately choose the kind of life Christ lived.

———— ❧ ————

Having outlined His own future, the Lord invited the disciples to follow Him. This would mean denying themselves and taking up their cross. To deny self means willingly to renounce any so-called right to plan or choose, and to recognize His lordship in every area of life. To take up the cross means to deliberately choose the kind of life He lived. This involves the opposition of loved ones, the reproach of the world, forsaking family and house and lands and the comforts of this life, complete dependence on God, obedience to the leading of the Holy Spirit, proclamation of an unpopular message, a pathway of loneliness, organized attacks from established religious leaders, suffering for righteousness' sake, slander and shame, pouring out one's life for others, and death to self and to the world. But it also involves laying hold of life itself. It means finding at last the reason for our existence and an eternal reward.

We instinctively recoil from a life of cross-bearing. Our minds are reluctant to believe this could be God's will for us. Yet the words of Christ "If anyone desires to come after Me . . ." mean "no person is excused and no one is excepted."

The natural tendency is to save our lives by selfish, complacent, routine, petty existences. We may indulge our pleasures and appetites, by basking in comfort, luxury, and ease, by living for the present, by trading our finest talents to the world in exchange for a few years of mock security. But in the very act we lose our lives by missing the true purpose of life and the profound spiritual pleasure it encompasses.

> **This life of abandonment is genuine living.**

On the other hand, we may lose our lives of the Savior's sake. Men think us mad if we fling our own selfish ambitions to the wind, by seeking first the kingdom of God and His righteousness, and yielding ourselves unreservedly to Him. But this life of abandonment is genuine living. It has a joy, a holy carefreeness, and a deep inward satisfaction defying description.

As the Savior talked with the Twelve, He realized the desire for material riches might be a powerful deterrent against full surrender. So He said, in effect, "Suppose you could stockpile all the gold and silver in the world, could own all the real estate and property, all the stocks and bonds—everything of material value. And suppose in your effort to acquire all this you missed the true purpose of life, what good would it do you? You would have it for only a short while; then you would leave it forever. It would be an insane bargain to sell that one, short life for a few toys of dust."

Another deterrent against total commitment to Christ is the fear of shame. It is completely irrational for a creature to be ashamed of his Creator, for a sinner to be ashamed of his Savior. Which of us is blameless? The Lord recognized the possibility of shame and solemnly warned against it. If we avoid the shame by nominal Christian lives, by conforming to the crowd, He will be ashamed of us when He comes in His own glory, in His Father's glory and in the glory of the holy angels. He emphasizes the triple-splendored glory of His second advent as if to say that any shame or reproach we may endure for Him now will seem trifling compared to the shame of those who deny Him when He appears in glory.

The mention of His glory in verse 26 forms the link with what follows. He now predicts that some of the disciples who were standing there would see the kingdom of God before they died. His words were fulfilled on the Mount of Transfiguration. The disciples were Peter, James, and John. On the Mount they saw a preview of what it will be like when the Lord Jesus sets up His kingdom on earth. Peter says this in effect in his second epistle that "we did not follow cunningly devised fables when we made known to you the power and coming of our Lord Jesus Christ, but were eyewitnesses of His majesty. For He received from God the Father honor and glory, when such a voice to Him from the Excellent Glory. 'This is My beloved Son, in whom I am well pleased.' And we heard this voice which came from heaven when we were with Him on the holy mountain" (2 Peter 1:16-18).

Notice the continuity of the Lord's teaching in this passage. He had announced His own impending rejection, suffering, and death. He had called His disciples to follow Him in a life of self-denial, suffering, and sacrifice. Now He says in effect, "But just remember! If you suffer with me, you will reign with me. Beyond the cross is the glory. The reward is all out of proportion to the cost." *thank you LORD JESUS*

The Transfiguration (9:28-36)

It was about eight days later when Jesus took Peter, James, and John up into a mountain to pray. The location of this mountain is unknown. As the Lord was praying His outward appearance began to change. An intriguing truth—that among the things that prayer changes is a man's countenance. His face glowed with a bright radiance and His clothing gleamed with dazzling whiteness. As mentioned above, this prefigured the glory which would be His during His coming kingdom. While God the Son was here on earth, His glory was ordinarily veiled in His body of flesh. He was here in humiliation, as a bond-slave. But during the millennium, His glory will be fully revealed. All will see Him in all His splendor and majesty.

"In the transfiguration, we have in miniature form all salient features of the future kingdom in manifestation. We see the Lord clothed in glory and not in the rags of humiliation. We behold Moses in a glorified state, the representative of the regenerated who have passed through death into the kingdom. We observe Elijah shrouded in glory, the representative of the redeemed who have entered the kingdom by translation. There are three disciples, Peter, James and John, who are not glorified—the representatives of Israel in the flesh during the millennium. Then there is the multitude at the foot of the mountain, representative of the nations who will be brought into the kingdom after it has been inaugurated" (Professor W. H. Rogers).

They talked with Jesus about the decease (or exodus) which He would accomplish at Jerusalem. Note His death is here spoken of as an accomplishment. Also note death is simply an exodus—not cessation of existence, but departure from one place to another one.

The disciples were sleepy while all this was going on. "Let it be noted that the very same disciples who here slept during a vision of glory were also found sleeping during the agony in the garden of Gethsemane. Flesh and blood does indeed need to be changed before it can enter heaven. Our poor weak bodies can neither watch with Christ in His time of trial nor keep awake with Him in His glorification. Our physical constitution must be greatly altered before we could enjoy heaven."[2]

When they awakened, they saw the bright outshining of Christ's glory. In an effort to preserve the sacred character of the occasion, Peter proposed erecting three tents or booths, one in honor of Jesus, one of Moses, and one of Elijah. But his idea was based upon zeal without knowledge. God's voice came out of a cloud that enveloped them, acknowledging Jesus as His beloved Son, and telling them to hear or obey Him. As soon as the voice was past, Moses and Elijah had disappeared. Jesus alone was standing there. It will be like this in the kingdom; He will have the preeminence in all things. He will not share His glory.

> In the kingdom, Jesus will have the preeminence in all things. He will not share His glory.

The disciples left with a sense of awe so profound that they did not discuss the event with any one else.

Jesus Casts Out the Unclean Spirit (9:37-43a)

From the mount of glory, Jesus and the disciples returned the next day to the valley of human need. Life has its moments of spiritual exaltation, but God balances them with the daily round of work and expenditure. From the multitude there came to meet them a distraught father, pleading for Jesus to help his demon-possessed son. It was his only child and therefore his heart's delight. What an unspeakable sorrow it was for the father to see his boy seized with demonic convulsions. These fits came on without warning. The lad would cry out and then foam at the mouth. Only after a fearful struggle did the demon depart, leaving him thoroughly bruised. The distressed father had previously gone to the disciples for help, but they were powerless. Why were the disciples unable to help the boy? Perhaps they had become "professional" in their ministry, thinking they could count on a Spirit-filled ministry without constant spiritual exercise. Perhaps they were taking things too much for granted.

The Lord Jesus was grieved by the entire spectacle. Without naming anyone in particular, He said, "O faithless and perverse generation . . ." This may have been addressed to the disciples, the people, the father, or all of them combined. They were all so helpless in the face of human need even though they could draw on His infinite resources of power. How long would He have to be with them and put up with them?

Then He said to the father, "Bring your son here." As the lad was coming to Jesus, he was seized by the demon and thrown to the ground violently. But Jesus was not overawed by this display of the power of an evil spirit; it was the unbelief of men hindering Him rather than the power of demonism. He cast out the evil spirit, healed the boy, and gave him back to his father. The people were amazed. They recognized that God had worked a miracle. They saw in the miracle a display of the majesty of God.

Jesus Predicts His Death (9:43b-45)

The disciples might be inclined to think that their Master would continue to perform miracles until at last the whole nation would acclaim Him as King. To disabuse their minds of such a notion, the Lord again reminded them that He must be delivered into the hands of men to be slain.

Why did they fail to understand this prediction? Simply because they lapsed back into thinking of the Messiah as a popular hero. Death would mean defeat for the cause, according to their thinking. Their own hopes were so strong that they were unable to entertain any contrary view. It was not God who concealed the truth from them, but their own determined refusal to believe. They were even afraid to ask for clarification—almost as if they were afraid to have their fears confirmed.

Greatness and Humility (9:46-48)

The disciples not only expected the glorious kingdom to be ushered in shortly, but also aspired to positions of greatness in the kingdom. Already they were arguing among themselves as to who was the greatest.

Knowing the question agitating them, Jesus brought a little child beside Him and explained that anyone who received a little child in His Name received Him. At first glance, this does not seem to have any connection with the question of who was great among the disciples. Though not obvious, the connection seems to be this: true greatness is seen in loving care for the little

> True greatness is seen in loving care for those who are helpless, for those whom the world passes by.

ones, for those who are helpless, for those whom the world passes by. Thus when Jesus said that "he who is least among you all will be great," He was referring to the one who humbled himself to associate with believers who are nondescript, insignificant, and despised.

In Matthew's gospel, the Lord said the greatest in the kingdom of heaven is the one who humbles himself like a little child (Matt. 18:4). Here in Luke, it is a matter of identifying oneself with the lowliest among God's children. In both cases, it involves taking a place of humiliation, as the Savior Himself did.

Help or Hindrance (9:49-50)

This incident seems to illustrate the behavior which the Lord had just told the disciples to avoid. They had found a man casting out demons in Jesus' name and forbade him for no better reason than that he was not one of their followers. In other words, they had refused to receive a child of the Lord in His Name. Instead of being sectarian and narrow, they should have been glad the demon had been cast out of the man. They should never be jealous of any man or group who casts out more demons than themselves. But then every disciple has to guard against this desire for exclusiveness, for a monopoly of spiritual power and prestige.

Jesus said, "Do not forbid him, for he who is not against us is on our side." This seems to contradict what we find in Matthew 12:30 and Luke 11:23. There we read the Lord Jesus when rebuking the Pharisees for blaspheming against the Holy Spirit said, "He who is not with Me is against Me." How can we explain this seeming contradiction?

It should be noticed in these latter two passages the wording is "with Me" and "against Me," whereas in Luke 9, it is "against us" and "on our side." In Matthew 12 and Luke 11, Christ is the issue. In Luke 9, the disciples are the issue, and it is a question of Christian service. As far as the Person and work of Christ are concerned, there can be no neutrality. If men are not for Christ, they are against Him. But when it comes to Christian service, "earnest Christians need to remember that when outsiders do anything in Christ's name, it must, on the whole, forward His cause . . ."

"The Master's reply contained a broad and far-reaching truth. No earthly society, however holy, would be able exclusively to claim the Divine powers inseparably connected with a true and faithful use of His Name" (A. L. Williams).

The Galilean ministry of our Lord closes at this point. The narrative from here to 19:28 covers the journey to Jerusalem.

The Spirit of Intolerance Rebuked (9:51-56)

The time of Jesus' ascension into heaven was now drawing near. He knew this well. He also knew the cross lay between, so He resolutely moved toward Jerusalem and what awaited Him there.

A Samaritan village on His route proved inhospitable to the Son of God. The people knew He was going to Jerusalem, and for them it was enough reason to bar Him. After all, there was intense hatred between the Samaritans and the Jews. Their sectarian, bigoted spirit, segregationist attitude, and racial pride made them unwilling to receive the Lord of Glory. James and John were so angered by this discourtesy that they offered to call lightning from heaven to destroy the offenders. Jesus promptly rebuked them. He had not come to destroy men's lives but to save them. This was the acceptable year of the Lord, not the day of vengeance of our God. They should have been characterized by grace, not vindictiveness.

Hindrances to Discipleship (9:57-62)

In these verses we meet some would-be disciples who illustrate three of the main hindrances to wholehearted discipleship.

The first man was quite sure he wanted to follow Jesus anywhere and everywhere. He did not wait to be called, but impetuously offered himself. He was self-confident, unduly eager, and unmindful of the cost. He did not know the meaning of what he said.

At first, the answer of Jesus does not seem to be related to the man's offer. However, there was a very close connection. Jesus was saying, in effect, "Do you know what it really means to follow Me? It means the forsaking of the comforts and conveniences of life. I do not have a home to call My own. This earth gives Me no rest. Foxes and birds have more in the way of natural comfort and security than I have. Are you willing to follow Me even if it means forsaking those things which most men consider to be their inalienable rights?"

When we read those words, ". . . the Son of Man has nowhere to lay His head," we are inclined to pity Him. One commentator remarks: "He does not need your pity. Pity yourself rather if you have a home that holds you back when Christ wants you out upon the high places of the world."

We hear no more of the man, and can only assume he was unwilling to give up the common comforts of life to follow the Lord Jesus.

The second man heard Christ's call to follow Him. He was willing, in a way, but there was something he wanted to do first. He wanted to go and bury his father.

Notice what he said. "Lord, let me first go . . ." In other words, "Lord . . . me first . . ." He called Jesus by the title "Lord" but actually he put his own desires and interests first. The words "Lord" and "me first" are totally opposed to each other; we must choose one or the other.

Whether the father was already dead or the son planned to wait at home until he died, the issue was the same: he was allowing something else to take precedence over Christ's call. It is perfectly legitimate and proper to show respect for a dead or dying father, but when anyone or anything is allowed to rival Christ, it becomes positively sinful.

This man had something else to do—we might say, a job or an occupation—and this lured him away from a pathway of unreserved discipleship. The Lord rebuked his double-mindedness with the words, "Let the dead bury their own dead, but you go and preach the kingdom of God." The spiritually dead can bury the physically dead, but they can't preach the gospel. Disciples should not give priority to tasks the unsaved can do just as well as Christians. The believer should make sure he is indispensable as far as the main thrust of his life is concerned. His principle occupation should be to advance the cause of Christ on earth.

The third would-be disciple resembled the first in that he volunteered to follow Christ. He was like the second in that he uttered the contradiction, "Lord . . . me first . . ." He wanted to say goodbye to his family. In itself, the request was reasonable and proper, but even the common civilities of life are wrong if they are placed ahead of prompt and complete obedience.

Jesus told him that once he put his hands to the plow of discipleship, he must not look back; otherwise he was not fit for the kingdom of God. Christ's followers are not made of half-hearted stuff or dreamy sentimentality. No considerations of family or friends, though lawful in themselves, must be allowed to turn them aside from utter and complete abandonment to Him.

The expression "fit for the kingdom of God" refers to service, not to salvation. It is not at all a question of entrance into the kingdom but of service in the kingdom after entering into it. Our fitness for entering into the kingdom is in the Person and work of the Lord Jesus. It becomes ours through faith in Him.

"The word 'look' can hardly mean a momentary glance back to see if the furrow is straight. Rather it implies a look with the intention of a change of mind and the abandoning of a task undertaken. It is a look with a wrong purpose" (C. G. Scorer).

We have three cardinal hindrances to discipleship illustrated in the experience of these men: material comforts, a job or an occupation, family and friends. Christ must reign in the heart without a rival. All other loves and loyalties must be secondary.

Jesus Commissions the Seventy (10:1-16)

This is the only account in the gospels of the Lord's sending out the seventy disciples. It closely resembles the commissioning of the twelve in Matthew 10. However, there the disciples were sent into the northern areas, whereas the seventy are now being sent to the south along the route the

Lord was following to Jerusalem. This mission was seemingly intended to prepare the way for the Lord in His journey from Caesarea Philippi in the north, through Galilee and Samaria, across the Jordan, south through Perea, then back across the Jordan to Jerusalem.

"The work [of the seventy] was for only a limited time and the office was temporary; but in His instructions to these men, Jesus suggested many principles of life which apply to His followers in all ages."

We might summarize some of these principles as follows.

➢ He sent them out by twos. This suggests competent testimony. "By the mouth of two or three witnesses every word shall be established" (2 Cor. 13:1).

➢ The Lord's servant should constantly pray that He will send forth laborers into His harvest field (v. 2). The need is always greater than the supply of workers. In praying for laborers, we must be willing to go ourselves, of course. Notice "pray" (v. 2) and "go" (v. 3).

➢ The disciples of Jesus are sent forth into a hostile environment (v. 3). They are, to outward appearances, like defenseless sheep in the midst of wolves. They cannot expect to be treated royally by the world, but rather to be persecuted and even slain.

➢ Considerations of personal comfort are not to be permitted (v. 4a). "Carry neither money bag, knapsack, nor sandals." The purse speaks of financial reserves. The knapsack (food-bag), suggests food reserves. The sandals may refer either to an extra pair or to footgear that provide more comfort than sandals. All three speak of the poverty which, though having nothing, yet possesses all things and makes many rich (2 Cor. 6:10).

➢ "Greet no one along the road" (v. 4b). Christ's servants are not to waste time on long, ceremonious greetings, such as were common in the East. While they should be courteous and civil, they must utilize their time in the glorious proclamation of the gospel rather than in profitless talk. There is no time for needless delays.

➢ They should accept hospitality wherever it is offered to them (vv. 5-6). If their initial greeting is favorably received, then the host is a son of peace—he is a man characterized by peace, and one who receives the message of peace. If the disciples are refused, they should not be discouraged; their peace has not been wasted or lost but will return to them again and others will receive it.

➤ The disciples should remain in the house that first offers lodging (v. 7). To move from one house to another might characterize them as those who are shopping for the most luxurious accommodations, whereas they should live simply and gratefully. They should not hesitate to eat whatever food and drink are offered to them. As servants of the Lord, they are entitled to their upkeep.

Cities and towns take a position either for or against the Lord, just as individuals do (vv. 8-9). If an area is receptive to the message, the disciple should preach there, accept its hospitality, and bring the blessings of the gospel to it. Christ's servants should eat such things as are set before them, not being fussy about their food or causing inconvenience in the home. After all, food is not the main thing in their lives.

> ───── ❧ ─────
> **Light rejected is light denied.**
> ───── ❧ ─────

Towns which receive the Lord's messengers still have their sin-sick inhabitants healed. Also the King draws very near to them (v. 9). A town may reject the gospel and then be denied the privilege of hearing it again (vv. 10-12). There comes a time in God's dealings when the message is heard for the last time. Men should not trifle with the gospel, because it may be withdrawn forever. Light rejected is light denied. Towns and villages which are privileged to hear the good news and which refuse it will be judged more severely than the city of Sodom. The greater the privilege, the greater the responsibility.

As Jesus spoke these words, He was reminded of three cities of Galilee which had been more highly privileged than any others. They had seen Him perform His mighty miracles in their streets. They had heard His gracious teaching. Yet they utterly refused Him.

If the miracles He had done in Chorazin and Bethsaida had been done in ancient Tyre and Sidon, those sea-coast cities would have plunged themselves into the deepest repentance. Because the cities of Galilee were unmoved by Jesus' works, their judgment would be more severe than that of Tyre and Sidon. As a matter of historical fact, Chorazin and Bethsaida have been so thoroughly destroyed that their exact location is not definitely known today.

Capernaum became the hometown of Jesus after He moved from Nazareth. The city was exalted to heaven in privilege. But it despised its most notable Citizen and missed its day of opportunity, so it was dashed down to Hades in judgment.

Jesus closed His instructions to the seventy with a statement about their being His ambassadors. To reject them was to reject Him, and to refuse God, the Father.

There is probably no stronger language than this in the New Testament about the dignity of a faithful minister's office, and the guilt incurred by those who refuse to hear his message. It is language, we must remember, which is not addressed to the twelve apostles, but to seventy disciples, of whose name and subsequent history we know nothing. Scott remarks, "To reject an ambassador, or to treat him with contempt, is an affront to the prince who commissioned and sent him, and whom he represents. The apostles and seventy disciples were the ambassadors and representatives of Christ; and they who rejected and despised them in fact rejected and despised Him."[3]

"Rejoice Not . . . Rejoice" (10:17-20)

As they returned from their mission, the seventy were elated that even the demons had been subject to them. Jesus' reply may be understood in two ways. First it may mean that He saw in their success an assurance of the eventual fall of Satan from heaven. Jamieson, Fausset and Brown paraphrase His words: "I followed you on your mission, and watched its triumphs; while you were wondering at the subjection to you of demons in My Name, a grander spectacle was opening to My view; sudden as the darting of lightning from heaven to earth, lo! Satan was beheld falling from heaven." This fall of Satan is still future. He will be cast out of heaven by Michael and his angels (Rev. 12:7-9). This will take place during the tribulation period, and prior to Christ's glorious reign on earth.

But there is a second possible interpretation of Jesus' words. They may be understood as a warning against pride, as if He were saying: "Yes, your heads are up in the clouds because even the demons have been subject to you. But just remember pride is the parent sin. It was pride that resulted in the fall of Lucifer, and in his being cast out of heaven. See that you avoid this peril."

The Lord had given His disciples authority against the forces of evil (v. 19). They were granted immunity from harm during their mission. It is true of all God's servants that they are immortal till their work is done. Yet they were not to rejoice in their power over demons, but rather in their own salvation. This is the only recorded instance when the Lord told His disciples not to rejoice. There are subtle dangers connected with success in Christian service, whereas the fact that our names are written in heaven reminds us of our infinite debt to God and to His Son. It is safe to rejoice in salvation by grace.

Hidden and Revealed (10:21-24)

Rejected by the mass of the people, Jesus looked upon His humble followers and rejoiced in the Holy Spirit, thanking the Father for His matchless wisdom. The seventy were not the wise and prudent men of this world. They were not the intellectuals or the scholars. They were mere babes. But they were babes with faith, with devotion and with unquestioning obedience. The intellectuals were too wise, too knowing, too clever for their own good. Their pride blinded them to the true worth of God's beloved Son. It is through babes that God can work most effectively. Our Lord was happy for all those whom the Father had given to Him, and for this initial success of the seventy, which foretold the eventual downfall of Satan.

All things were delivered to the Son by the Father, whether things in heaven, on earth or under the earth. God put the entire universe under the authority of His Son. No one knows who the Son is but the Father. There is mystery connected with the incarnation that no one but the Father can fathom. How God could become Man and dwell in a human body is beyond the comprehension of the creature. No one knows who the Father is but the Son, and those to whom the Son chooses to reveal Him. God too is above human understanding. The Son knows Him perfectly, and the Son has revealed Him to the weak, the lowly, and the despised people who have faith in Him (1 Cor. 1:26-29). Those who have seen the Son have seen the Father. The only begotten Son who is in the bosom of the Father has fully revealed the Father (John 1:18).

Kelly says, "The Son does reveal the Father; but men's mind always breaks itself to pieces when he attempts to unravel the insoluble enigma of Christ's personal glory."

In private, the Lord Jesus told the disciples that they were living in a day of unprecedented privilege. Old Testament kings and prophets had yearned to see the days of the Messiah, but had not seen them. The Lord Jesus here claims to be the One to whom the Old Testament prophets looked forward—the Messiah. The disciples were privileged to witness the miracles and hear the teaching of the Hope of Israel.

The Lawyer and the Good Samaritan (10:25-37)

The lawyer, an expert in the teachings of the law of Moses, was not sincere in his question. He was trying to trick Jesus, to put Him thoroughly to the test. Perhaps he thought the Lord would repudiate the law. To him, Jesus was only a Teacher, and eternal life was something he could earn or merit.

Jesus took all this into consideration when He answered him. If the lawyer had been humble and penitent, Jesus would have answered him more directly. Under the circumstances, Jesus directed his attention to the law. What did the law demand? It demanded that man love God supremely, and his neighbor as himself. Jesus told him that if he did this, he would live.

> God never intended that anyone should ever be saved by keeping the law.

At first, it might appear Jesus was teaching salvation by law-keeping. Such was not the case. God never intended that anyone should ever be saved by keeping the law. The Ten Commandments were given to people who were already sinners. The purpose of the law was not to save from sin, but to produce the knowledge of sin. The function of the law is to show man what a guilty sinner he is.

It is impossible for sinful man to love God with all his heart, and his neighbor as himself. If he could do this from birth to death, he would not need salvation. He would not be lost. But even then, his reward would only be long life on earth, not eternal life in heaven. As long as he lived sinlessly, he would go on living. Eternal life is only for sinners who acknowledge their lost condition and who are saved by God's grace.

Thus Jesus' statement, "Do this and you will live," was purely hypothetical. If His reference to the law had had its desired effect on the lawyer he would have said, "If that's what God requires, then I'm lost, helpless, and hopeless. I cast myself on Your love and mercy. Save me by Your grace."

Instead, he sought to justify himself. Why justify himself, bearing in mind no one had accused him of anything. Because he was conscious of being at fault and his heart rose up in its pride to defend itself. He therefore asked, "Who is my neighbor?" It was an evasive tactic on his part.

It was in answer to this question that the Lord Jesus told the story of the good Samaritan. The details of the story are familiar. The robbery-victim (almost certainly a Jew) lay half dead on the road to Jericho. The Jewish priest and Levite refused to help; perhaps they feared it was a plot, or were afraid that they too might be robbed if they stayed to help him. It was a hated Samaritan who came to the rescue, who applied first aid, who took the victim to an inn, and who made provision for his care. To the Samaritan, a Jew in need was his neighbor.

Then Jesus asked the inescapable question, Which of the three proved to be a neighbor to the helpless man? The one who showed mercy, of course. Yes, of course. Then the lawyer should go and do likewise. "If a Samaritan could prove himself a true neighbor to a Jew by showing mercy to him, then all men are neighbors."⁴

It is not difficult for us to see in the priest and Levite a picture of the powerlessness of the law to help the dead sinner. The law commanded "Love your neighbor as yourself," but it did not give the power to obey. Neither is it difficult to identify the kind Samaritan with the Lord Jesus who came to where we were, saved us from our sins, and made full provision for us from earth to heaven and through all eternity.

The story had an unexpected twist to it. It started off to answer the question, "Who is my neighbor?" But it ended by posing the question, "To whom do you prove yourself a neighbor?"

Mary and Martha (10:38-42)

Both Darby and Kelly point out that Jesus now centered His attention on the word of God and prayer as the two great means of blessing (10:38-11:54).

Mary sat at the Lord's feet and heard His teaching, while Martha was distracted by her preparations for the Royal Guest. Martha wanted Jesus to rebuke her sister for failing to help, but Jesus tenderly rebuked Martha for her fretfulness.

Our Lord prizes our affection above our service. Service may be tainted with pride and self-importance. Occupation with Himself is the one needful thing, the good part which shall not be taken away. "The Lord wants to convert us from Marthas into Marys, just as He wants to convert us from lawyers into neighbors."[5]

"While the Master does appreciate all that we undertake for Him, He knows that our first need is to sit at His feet and learn His will; then in our tasks we shall be calm and peaceful and kindly, and at last our service may attain the perfectness of that Mary when in a later scene she poured upon the feet of Jesus the ointment, the perfume of which still fills the world."[6]

In ourtasks we shall be
calm
peaceful
kindly
at last our service may attain
the perfectness of that mary
who poured the ointment on Jesus
feet
the perfume of which still
fills the world.

[1] James S. Stewart, *op. cit.*, pp. 109, 110.
[2] James Charles Ryle, *op. cit.*, p. 320.
[3] James Charles Ryle, *op. cit.*, pp. 357, 358.
[4] F. Davidson (ed.), *The New Bible Commentary* (Chicago: Inter-Varsity Christian Fellowship, 1953) p. 851.
[5] C. A. Coates, *An Outline of Luke's Gospel* (Kingston on Thames: Stow Hill Bible and Tract Depot, n.d.) p. 129.
[6] Charles R. Erdman, *The Gospel of Luke* (Philadelphia: The Westminster Press, 1929) p. 112.

6

TEACHINGS OF JESUS
(11:1–12:59)

Teach Us to Pray (11:1-4)

The time interval between chapters 10 and 11 is covered in John 9–10:21. This is another of the frequent references by Luke to the prayer life of the Lord Jesus. It fits in with Luke's purpose in presenting Him as the Son of Man, ever dependent upon God His Father. The disciples sensed that prayer was a real and vital force in the life of Jesus. As they heard Him pray, it made them want to pray as well, so one of the disciples asked if He would teach them to pray. It has often been pointed out that He did not say, "Teach us how to pray," but "Teach us to pray." However, the request certainly includes both the fact and the method.

> Prayer was a real and vital force in the life of Jesus.

The model prayer which Jesus gave to them at this time is somewhat different from the so-called Lord's Prayer in Matthew's gospel. These differences all have a purpose and meaning. None of them is without significance.

First, the Lord taught the disciples to address God as Father. This intimate family relationship was unknown to believers in the Old Testament. It simply means that believers are now to speak to God as to a loving heavenly Father. Next, we are taught to pray that God's name should be hallowed. This expresses the longing of the believer's heart of reverencing, magnifying, and adoring Him. In the petition, "Your kingdom come," we have a prayer that the day will soon arrive when God will put down the forces of evil and, in the Person of Christ, reign supreme over the earth.

Having thus sought first the kingdom of God and His righteousness, the petitioner is taught to make known his personal needs and desires. The ever-recurring need for food, both physical and spiritual, is introduced. We are to live in daily dependence upon Him, acknowledging Him as the source of every good thing. Next there is the prayer for the forgiveness of sins, based upon the fact that we have shown a forgiving spirit to others. Obviously this does not refer to forgiveness from the penalty of sin which is based upon the finished work of Christ on Calvary's cross, and is received through faith alone. What we are dealing with here is parental, or governmental, forgiveness. After we are saved, God deals with us as with children. If He finds a hard and unforgiving spirit in our hearts, He will chastise us until we are broken and brought back into fellowship with Himself. The forgiveness spoken of in verse 4 has to do with fellowship with God, rather than with relationship.

The prayer "do not lead us into temptation" presents difficulties to some. We know God never tempts anyone to sin. But He does allow us to experience trials and testings in life, and these are designed for our good. Here the thought seems to be that we should constantly be aware of our own propensity to wander and fall into sin. We should ask the Lord to keep us from falling into sin, even if we ourselves might want to do it. We should pray that the opportunity to sin and the desire to do so should never coincide. The prayer expresses a healthy distrust of our own ability to resist temptation.

Ask . . . Seek . . . Knock (11:5-13)

Continuing with the subject of prayer, the Lord gave an illustration designed to show God's willingness to hear and answer the petitions of His children. The story has to do with a man who had a guest arrive at his home late at night. Unfortunately he did not have enough food on hand. So he went to a neighbor, knocked on his door, and asked for three loaves of bread. At first the neighbor was annoyed by the interruption to his sleep and didn't bother to get up. Yet because of the prolonged banging and shouting of the worried host, he finally did get up and give him what he needed.

In applying this illustration we must be careful to avoid certain conclusions. It doesn't mean that God is annoyed by our persistent requests. And it doesn't suggest the only way to get our prayers answered is to be persistent. It does teach if a man is willing to help a friend because of his importunity, God is much more willing to hear the cries of His children.

It teaches we should not grow weary or discouraged in our prayer life. "Keep on asking . . . keep on seeking . . . keep on knocking . . ." is the literal translation. Sometimes God answers our prayers the first time we ask, but in other cases He answers only after prolonged asking. It seems to teach increasing degrees of importunity—from asking to seeking to knocking.

The teaching is that everyone who asks receives, everyone who seeks finds, and everyone who knocks has it opened to him. This is a promise that when we pray, God always gives us what we ask or something better. A "no" answer means He knows that our request would not be the best for us; His denial is then better than our petition.

It teaches that God will never deceive us by giving us a stone when we ask bread. Bread in those days was shaped in a round flat cake, often resembling a stone. God will never mock us by giving us something inedible when we ask for food. If we ask for a fish, He will not give us a serpent, or something that might destroy us. And if we ask for an egg, He will not give us a scorpion, something causing excruciating pain. A human father would not do this; even though he has a sinful nature, he knows how to give good gifts to his children. How much more is our Father in heaven willing to give the Holy Spirit to those who ask Him. "It is significant that the gift He selects as the one we most need, and the one He most desires to give, is the Holy Spirit" (J. G. Bellett).

When Jesus spoke these words, the Holy Spirit had not yet been given (John 7:39). We would not pray today for the Holy Spirit to be given to us as an indwelling Person, because He comes to indwell us at the time of our conversion (Rom. 8:9b; Eph. 1:13-14). But it is certainly proper and necessary for us to pray for the Holy Spirit in other ways. We should pray that we will be receptive to the teachings of the Holy Spirit. We should pray that we will be guided by the Spirit. And we should pray that His power will be poured out on us in all our service for Christ.

It is quite possible that when Jesus taught the disciples to ask for the Holy Spirit, He was referring to the ministry of the Holy Spirit to enable them to live the other worldly type of discipleship that He had been teaching in the preceding chapters. By this time, they were probably feeling how utterly impossible it was for them to meet the tests of discipleship in their own strength. This is, of course, true. The Holy Spirit enables one to live the Christian life. This is why Jesus pictured God as anxious to give this power to those who ask.

It has been pointed out that in the original language of the New Testament, verse 13 does not say that God will give *the* Holy Spirit, but rather He will give Holy Spirit (without the article). Professor H. B. Swete pointed out that when the article is present, it refers to the Person Himself. When the article is absent, it refers to His gifts or operations on our behalf. So in this passage, it is not so much a prayer for the Person of the Holy Spirit, but rather for His ministries in our lives.

Jesus Answers His Critics (11:14-26)

When Jesus cast out the demon responsible for its victim's dumbness, it created quite a stir among the people. While some marveled, others become more openly opposed to Him. The opposition took two main forms. Some accused Him of casting out demons by the power of Beelzebub, the prince of demons. Others suggested He should perform a miracle from heaven; perhaps their idea was that this might disprove the charge made against Him.

The accusation that He cast out demons because He was indwelt by Beelzebub is answered in verses 17-26. The request for a sign is answered in verse 29. First of all, the Lord Jesus reminded them that a kingdom divided against itself is destroyed, and a house divided against itself falls. If He was a tool of Satan in casting out demons, then Satan was fighting against his own underlings. It is ridiculous to think the devil would oppose himself and obstruct his own purposes.

Second, the Lord reminded His critics that some of their own countrymen even then were casting out evil spirits. If *He* did it by the power of Satan, it necessarily follows they must be doing it by the same power. The Jews would never be willing to admit this. Yet how could they deny the force of the argument? The power to cast out demons came either from God or from Satan. It had to be one or the other; it could not be both. If Jesus acted by the power of Satan, then the Jewish exorcists depended upon the same power. To condemn Him was to condemn them also.

The true explanation is that Jesus cast out demons by "the finger of God" (v. 20). What did He mean by the finger of God? In the account in Matthew's gospel (12:28), we read: "But if I cast out demons by the Spirit of God, surely the kingdom of God has come upon you." So we conclude that the finger of God is the same as the Spirit of God.

The fact that Jesus was casting out demons by the Spirit of God was evidence that the kingdom of God had come upon the people of that generation. The kingdom had come in the Person of the King Himself. The very fact that the Lord Jesus was there, performing such miracles, was positive proof that God's anointed Ruler had appeared upon the stage of history.

Up until now, Satan was a strong one, fully armed, who held undisputed sway over his court. Those who were possessed by demons were kept in his grip with no one to challenge him. His "goods" were in peace because no one had the power to dispute his sway. The Lord Jesus was stronger than Satan, came upon him, overcame him, took his arms, and divided his spoil. Not even Jesus' critics denied He was casting out evil spirits. This could only mean Satan had been conquered and his victims were being liberated. This is the point of verses 21 and 22.

Then Jesus added that anyone who is not with Him is against Him, and anyone who does not gather with Him scatters. As someone has said, "A man is either on the way or in the way." We have already mentioned the seeming contradiction between this verse and 9:50. If the issue is the Person and work of Christ, there can be no neutrality. A man who is not for Christ is against Him. But when it is a matter of Christian service, those who are not against Christ's servants are for them. In the first verse, it is a matter of salvation, in the second a matter of service.

In verses 24-26 the Lord is turning the tables on His Jewish critics. They had accused Him of being demon possessed. He now likens their nation to a man who had been temporarily cured of demon-possession. This was true in their history. Prior to the captivity, the nation of Israel had been possessed with the "demon" of idolatry. But the captivity rid them of this evil spirit. Since then, the Jews have never been given over to idolatry. Their house has been swept and in good order, but they have refused to let the Lord Jesus come in and take possession. Therefore He predicted that in a coming day the evil spirit would gather seven other spirits more wicked than himself, enter into the house and dwell therein. This refers to the terrible form of idolatry that the Jewish nation will adopt during the tribulation period, when they will acknowledge the antichrist to be God (John 5:43). The punishment for this sin will be greater than the nation has ever endured before.

While this illustration refers primarily to Israel's national history, it also points up the insufficiency of mere repentance or reformation in an individual's life. It is not enough to turn over a new leaf. The Lord Jesus

Christ must be welcomed into the heart and life. Otherwise the life is open to entrance by more vile forms of sin than ever indulged in before.

More Blessed than Mary (11:27-28)

An unnamed woman came out of the crowd to salute Jesus with the words, "Blessed is the womb that bore You, the breasts which nursed You!" The reply of our Lord was most significant. He did not deny that His mother, Mary, was blessed, but He went beyond this and said it was even more important to hear the word of God and to do it. Even the virgin Mary was more blessed in believing on Christ and following Him than she was in being His mother. Natural relationship is not as important as spiritual. This should be sufficient to silence those who would make Mary an object of worship.

An Evil Generation (11:29-32)

In verse 16, some had tempted the Lord Jesus by asking for a sign from heaven. He now answers by ascribing the request to an evil generation. He was primarily speaking about the Jewish generation that was living at the time. The people had been privileged with the presence of the Son of God. They had heard His words, and had witnessed His miracles. But they were not satisfied with this. They now pretended they would believe on Him if they could only see a mighty, supernatural work in the heavens.

Jesus answered that no further sign would be given to them except the sign of the prophet Jonah. He was referring to His own resurrection from the dead. Just as Jonah was delivered from the sea after being in the fish's belly for three days and three nights, the Lord Jesus would rise from the dead after being in the grave for three days and three nights. The last and conclusive miracle in the earthly ministry of the Lord Jesus would be His resurrection.

Jonah was a sign to the Ninevites. When he went to preach to this Gentile nation, he went as one who figuratively had risen from the dead.

The Queen of the South was the Queen of Sheba. This Gentile ruler traveled a great distance to hear the wisdom of Solomon. She did not see a single miracle. If she had been privileged to live in the days of the Lord, how readily she would have received Him. Therefore she will rise up in the judgment against those wicked men who were privileged to see the supernatural works of the Lord Jesus who still rejected Him.

A greater than Jonah or Solomon had stepped upon the stage of human history. The men of Nineveh repented at the preaching of Jonah, but the men of Israel refused to repent at the preaching of a greater than Jonah.

Unbelief today scoffs at the story of Jonah, assigning it to ancient mythology. Jesus spoke of Jonah as an actual person of history, just as He spoke of Solomon. People who say they would believe if they could see a miracle are mistaken. Faith is not based on the evidences of the senses but on the living Word of God. If a man will not believe the Word of God, he will not believe though one should rise from the dead. The attitude that demands a sign is not pleasing to God. That is not faith, but sight. Unbelief says, "Let me see and then I will believe." God says, "Believe and then you will see."

> Faith is not based on the evidences of the senses but on the living Word of God.

Light and Darkness (11:33-36)

At first we might be tempted to think there is no connection between these verses and the preceding ones. But on closer examination we find a very vital link. The Lord Jesus reminded His hearers that no man puts a lighted lamp in the cellar or under a bushel basket. He puts it on a stand where it will be seen and provide light for all who enter.

The application is this. God is the One who has lighted the lamp. In the Person and work of the Lord Jesus, He provided a blaze of illumination for the world. If any man doesn't see the Light, it isn't God's fault. There are two hindrances to the shining forth of the light: the cellar and the bushel. The cellar is a secret place, and speaks of man's unwillingness to come to Christ (the Light) because of fear, shame, and reproach. The bushel speaks of business and the covetousness so often associated with it. The two hindrances to the shining of the light in men's hearts are the cellar of shame and the bushel of business. Our Lord had already warned His disciples against these perils in 9:25-26.

Verse 33 seems to be a repetition of 8:16. However, in chapter 8, Jesus was speaking of the responsibility of those who were already His disciples to propagate the faith and not to hide it under the bushel of business or the bed of laziness. Here in 11:33 He is exposing the unbelief of His sign-seeking critics as caused by their covetousness and fear of shame. Verse 34 further underscores the fact that their unbelief was a result of their impure motives.

In the physical realm, the eye is what gives light to the whole body. If the eye is healthy, then the person can see the light. But if the eye is diseased or blind, then the light cannot get in. It is the same in the spiritual realm. If a person is sincere in his desire to know if Jesus is the Christ of God, then God will reveal it to him. But if his motives are not pure and he wants to cling to his covetousness, fearing what others will say, then he is blinded to the true worth of the Lord Jesus Christ.

> If a person is sincere in his desire to know if Jesus is the Christ of God, then God will reveal it to him.

The men whom Jesus was addressing thought themselves to be very wise. They supposed they had a great deal of light. But the Lord Jesus warned them to consider the fact that their light was actually darkness. Their own pretended wisdom and superiority kept them from Him (v. 35).

Verse 36 teaches that the person whose motives are pure, who opens His complete being to Jesus, the Light of the world, this person is flooded with spiritual illumination. His inward life is enlightened by Christ just as his body is illuminated when he sits in the direct rays of a lamp.

Outward and Inward Cleanliness (11:37-41)

When Jesus accepted a Pharisee's invitation to dinner, His host was shocked that He had not first bathed Himself before eating. Jesus read his thoughts and thoroughly rebuked him for such hypocrisy and externalism. Jesus reminded him that what really counts is not the cleanliness of the outside of a dish but the inside. Outwardly the Pharisees appeared quite righteous, but inwardly they were crooked and wicked. The same God who made the outside of man made the inside as well, and He wants our inward lives to be pure. Man looks on the outward appearance, but God looks on the heart (1 Sam. 16:7).

The Lord Jesus realized how covetous and selfish these Pharisees were, so He told His host first to give for alms such things as he had. If he could pass this basic test of love to others, then all things would be clean unto him.

"When the love of God fills the heart so that one will be concerned about the needs of others, then only will these outward observances have any real value. He who is constantly gathering up for himself, in utter indifference to the poor and needy about him, gives evidence that the love of God does not dwell in him."[1]

Someone has well said, "The severe things said in verses 39-52 against Pharisees and lawyers were said at a Pharisee's dinner table (v. 37). What we call 'good taste' is often made a substitute for loyalty to truth; we smile when we should frown; and we are silent when we should speak. Better break up a dinner party than break faith with God."

Jesus Rebukes the Pharisees (11:42-44)

The Pharisees were externalists. They were punctilious about the smallest details of the ceremonial law, such as tithing tiny herbs. But they were quite careless in their relations with God and with man. They oppressed the poor and failed to love God. Jesus did not rebuke them for tithing mint and rue and every herb, but simply pointed out that they should not be so zealous in this particular and neglect the basic duties of life, such as justice and love. They emphasized the subordinate but overlooked the primary. They excelled in what could be seen by others but were careless about what only God could see.

They loved to parade themselves, to occupy positions of prominence in the religious world, and to attract as much attention as possible in public life. They were thus guilty not only of externalism but of pride as well.

Finally the Lord compared them to unmarked tombs. Under the law of Moses, whoever touched a grave was unclean for seven days (Num. 19:16), even if he didn't know at the time it was a grave. The Pharisees outwardly gave the appearance of being devout religious leaders. But they should have worn a sign warning people it was defiling to come in touch with them. They were like unmarked graves, full of corruption and uncleanness, and infecting others with their externalism and pride.

Jesus Denounces the Lawyers (11:45-52)

The lawyers were the scribes—experts in explaining and interpreting the law of Moses. However, their skill was limited to telling others what to do. They did not practice it themselves.

One of the lawyers had felt the cutting edge of Jesus' words, and reminded Him that in criticizing the Pharisees, He was also insulting them. The Lord used this as an occasion to lash out at some of the sins of the lawyers. First, they oppressed the people with all kinds of legal burdens, but did nothing to help them bear these burdens. "They were notorious for their contempt of the very people from whom they derived their importance."[2] Many of their rules were man-made and were concerned with matters of no real importance.

The lawyers were hypocritical murderers. They pretended to admire the prophets of God. They went so far as to erect monuments over the graves of the Old Testament prophets. This certainly seemed to be a proof of deep respect. But the Lord Jesus knew differently. While outwardly dissociating themselves from their Jewish ancestors who killed the prophets, they were actually following their footsteps. At the very time they were building sepulchers for the prophets, they were plotting the death of God's greatest Prophet, the Lord Himself. And they would continue to murder God's faithful prophets and apostles.

By comparing verse 49 with Matthew 23:34, it will be seen that Jesus Himself is the wisdom of God. Here He quotes the wisdom of God as saying, "I will send them prophets . . ." In Matthew's gospel He does not give this as a quotation from the Old Testament or from any other source, but simply presents it as His own statement. (See also 1 Corinthians 1:30 where Christ is spoken of as wisdom.)

The Lord Jesus promised He would send prophets and apostles to the men of His generation, and the latter would persecute and kill them. He would require of that generation the blood of all God's spokesmen, beginning with the first recorded case in the Old Testament, that of Abel, down to the last instance, that of Zechariah who perished between the altar and the sanctuary (2 Chron. 24:21). Second Chronicles was the last book in the Jewish Old Testament; the Lord Jesus therefore ran the entire gamut of martyrs when He mentioned Abel and Zechariah.

As He spoke these words, He well knew the generation then living would put Him to death on the cross of Calvary, and thus bring to an awful climax all their previous persecution of men of God. It was because they would murder Him that all the blood of previous dispensations would fall upon them.

Finally, the Lord Jesus denounced the lawyers for taking away the key of knowledge, withholding God's written Word from the people. Though outwardly they professed loyalty to the Scriptures, yet they stubbornly refused to receive the One of whom the Scriptures spoke. And they did everything in their power to hinder others from coming to Christ. They didn't want Him themselves, and like the proverbial dog in the manger, they didn't want others to receive Him.

Traps Laid for Jesus (11:53-54)

The Pharisees and scribes were obviously angered by the Lord's straightforward accusations. They began to jostle Him, and stepped up their efforts to trap Him in His words. By every possible device, they sought to trick Him into saying something for which they could condemn Him to death. In doing so, they only proved how accurately He had read their characters.

Warnings and Encouragements (12:1-12)

A large crowd had gathered while Jesus was condemning the Pharisees and lawyers. A dispute or a debate will generally attract a throng, but this crowd was also drawn, no doubt, by Jesus' fearless denunciation of these hypocritical religious leaders. Although an uncompromising attitude toward sin is not always popular, yet it commends itself to the heart of man as being righteous. Truth is always self-verifying.

Turning to the disciples, the Lord Jesus warned them to beware of the leaven of the Pharisees. He explained that leaven is a symbol or picture of hypocrisy. A hypocrite is one who wears a mask, one whose outward appearance is utterly different from what he is inwardly. The Pharisees posed as paragons of virtue but actually were masters of masquerade. Their day of exposure would come. All they had concealed would be revealed, and all they had done in darkness would be dragged out into the light.

Just as inevitable as the unmasking of hypocrisy is the triumph of truth. Up to then, the message proclaimed by the disciples had been spoken in relative obscurity and to limited audiences. But following the rejection of the Messiah by Israel, and the coming of the Holy Spirit, the disciples would go forth fearlessly in the Name of the Lord Jesus and proclaim the good news far and wide. Then it would be proclaimed upon the housetops, comparatively speaking. "Those whose voice cannot now find a hearing, save within limited, obscure circles, shall become the teachers of the world."[3]

"And I say to you, My friends" (v. 4). With these words of encouragement and endearment, Jesus warns His disciples not to be ashamed of this priceless friendship under any trials. The worldwide proclamation of the Christian message would bring persecution and death to the loyal disciples. But there was a limit to what men like the Pharisees could do to them. Physical death was that limit. They should not fear this. God would visit their persecutors with a far worse punishment, namely, eternal death in hell. The disciples were to fear God rather than man.

> **The disciples were to fear God rather than men.**

To emphasize God's protective interest in the disciples, the Lord Jesus mentioned the Father's care for sparrows (v. 6). In Matthew 10:29 we read that two sparrows are sold for a farthing. Here we learn that five sparrows are sold for two farthings. In other words, an extra sparrow is thrown in free when four are purchased. Yet not even this odd sparrow with no commercial value is forgotten in the sight of God. If God cares for an odd sparrow, how much more does He watch over those who go forth with the gospel of His Son. He numbers the hairs of their heads.

Jesus told the disciples that all who confess Him now will be confessed by Him before the angels of God. Here He is speaking of all true believers. To confess Him is to receive Him as only Lord and Savior. Those who deny Him before men will be denied before the angels of God. The primary reference here seems to be to the Pharisees, but the verse also includes all who refuse Christ and are ashamed to acknowledge Him. In that day, He will say, "I never knew you."

Next, Jesus explained to the disciples that there is a difference between criticism of Him and blasphemy against the Holy Spirit (v. 10). Those who speak against Christ can be forgiven if they repent and believe. But blasphemy against the Holy Spirit is the unpardonable sin. This is the sin of which the Pharisees were guilty (see Matthew 12:22-32). What is this sin? It is the sin of attributing the miracles of the Lord Jesus to the devil. It is blasphemy against the Holy Spirit because Jesus performed all His miracles in the power of the Holy Spirit. Therefore, it was in effect saying that the Holy Spirit of God is the devil. There is no forgiveness for this sin in this age or in the age to come.

The sin cannot be committed by a true believer, though some are tortured by fears that they have committed it by backsliding. Backsliding is not the unpardonable sin; any backslider can be restored to fellowship with the Lord. The very fact a person is concerned is evidence he has not committed the unpardonable sin.

Rejection of Christ by an unbeliever is not the unforgivable sin either. A person may spurn the Savior repeatedly, yet he may later turn to the Lord and be converted. Of course, if he dies in unbelief, he can no longer be forgiven. His sin then, in fact, becomes unpardonable. But the sin which our Lord described as unpardonable is what the Pharisees committed by saying He performed His miracles by the power of Beelzebub, the prince of the demons.

It was inevitable that the disciples would be brought before governmental authorities for trial. The Lord Jesus told them it was unnecessary for them to rehearse in advance what they would say. The Holy Spirit would put the proper words in their mouths whenever it was necessary. This does not mean servants of the Lord should not spend time in prayer and study before preaching the gospel or teaching the Word of God. This is no excuse for laziness. However, it is a definite promise from the Lord to those placed on trial for their witness for Christ of special help from God's Spirit. And it is a general promise to all God's people that if they walk in the Spirit, they will be given the suitable words to speak in the crisis moments of life.

The Sin of Covetousness (12:13-21)

A man stepped out from the crowd and asked the Lord to settle a dispute between his brother and himself over an inheritance. It has often been said that where there's a will, there are a lot of relatives. This seems to be a case in point.

> The insatiable lust for material possessions completely misses the purpose of life.

We are not told whether the man was being deprived of his rightful portion, or whether he was greedy for more than his share.

Jesus quickly reminded him that He had not come into the world to handle such trivial matters. The purpose of His coming involved the salvation of sinful men and women. He would not be deflected from this grand and glorious mission to divide a pitiful inheritance. (In addition, He did not have legal authority to judge matters involving estates. His decisions would not have been binding.)

But the Lord did use this incident to warn His hearers against one of the most insidious evils of the human heart, namely, covetousness (v. 15). The insatiable lust for material possessions is one of the strongest drives in all of life, and yet it completely misses the purpose of human existence. A man's life does not consist in the abundance of his possessions.

"This is one of the red flags our Lord hung out which most people nowadays do not seem much to regard. Christ said a great deal about the danger of riches; but not many persons are afraid of riches. Covetousness is not practically considered a sin in these times. If a man breaks the sixth or eighth commandment, he is branded as a criminal and covered with shame; but he may break the tenth, and he is only enterprising. The Bible says the love of money is a root of all evil; but every man who quotes the saying puts a terrific emphasis on the word 'love,' explaining that it is not money, but only the love of it, that is such a prolific root.

"To look about one, one would think a man's life *did* consist in the abundance of the things he possesses. Men think they become great just in proportion as they gather wealth. So it seems, too; for the world measures men by their bank account. Yet there never was a more fatal error. A man is really measured by what he *is*, and not by what he *has*."[4]

The parable of the rich fool illustrates the fact that possessions are not the principal thing in life. Because of an exceptionally good crop, this wealthy farmer was faced with what seemed a very distressing problem. He did not know what to do with all the grain. All his barns and silos were crammed to capacity. Then he had a brainwave. He decided to tear down his barns and build bigger ones. He could have saved himself the expense and bother of this tremendous construction project if he had just looked on the needy world about him, and used these possessions to satisfy hunger, both spiritual and physical. "The bosoms of the poor, the houses of widows, the mouths of children are the barns which last forever" (Ambrose).

As soon as his new barns were built, he planned to retire. Notice his spirit of independence: my barns, my fruits, my goods, my soul. He had the future all planned. He was going to take his ease, eat, drink, and be merry. "But when he began to think of time as his, he crashed into God to his eternal ruin." God told him he would die that very night. Then he would lose ownership of all his material possessions. They would fall to someone else.

Someone has defined a fool as one whose plans end at the grave. This man surely was a fool. "Then whose will those things be?" (v. 20). We might well ask ourselves the question, "If Christ should come today, whose would all my possessions be?" How much better to use them for God today than to let them fall into the devil's hands tomorrow! We can lay up treasure in heaven with them now, and thus be rich toward God. Or we can squander them on our flesh, and of the flesh reap corruption.

Anxiety and Faith (12:22-34)

One of the great dangers in the Christian life is that the acquisition of food and clothing becomes the first and foremost aim of our existence. We become so occupied with earning money for these things that the work of the Lord is relegated to a secondary place. The emphasis of the New Testament is that the cause of Christ should have first place in our lives. Food and clothing should be subordinate. We should work hard for the supply of our current necessities, then trust God for the future as we plunge ourselves into His service. This is the life of faith.

When the Lord Jesus said we should not be anxious for food and clothing, He did not mean we were to sit idly and wait for these things to be provided. Christianity does not encourage laziness. But He certainly did mean in the process of earning money for the necessities of life, we were not to let them assume undue importance. After all, there is something more important in life than what we eat and what we wear. We are here as ambassadors of the King, and all considerations of personal comfort and appearance must be subordinated to the one glorious task of making Him known.

The Lord Jesus used the ravens as an example of how God cares for His creatures. They do not spend their lives in a frantic quest for food and in providing for future needs. They live in hourly dependence upon God. The fact that they do not sow or reap should not be stretched to teach that men should refrain from secular occupations. All it means is that God knows the needs of those whom He has created, and He will supply them if we walk in dependence on Himself. If God feeds the ravens, how much more will He feed those whom He has created, whom He has saved by His grace, and whom He has called to be His servants. The ravens have no barns or storehouses, yet God provides for them on a daily basis. Why then should we spend our lives building bigger barns and storage bins?

In verse 25, Jesus asked, "Which of you by worrying can add one cubit to his stature?" This indicates the folly of worrying over things (such as the future) over which we have no control. No one by worrying can add to his height, or to the length of his life. Why worry about the future then? Rather, let us use our strength and time serving Christ, and leave the future to Him. (The expression "his stature" is translated "the measure of his life" in the American Standard Version. It may refer to length of life rather than to height.)

> Let us use our strength and time serving Christ.

The lilies are next introduced to show the folly of spending one's finest talents in the obtaining of clothes. The lilies of the field are probably wild anemones. They neither toil nor spin, yet they have a natural beauty which rivals Solomon in all his glory. If God lavishes such beauty on flowers which bloom today and are burned tomorrow, will He be unmindful of the needs of His children? We prove ourselves to be of little faith when we worry, fret, and rush around in a ceaseless struggle to get more and more material possessions. We waste our lives doing that which God would have done for us, if we had only devoted our time and talents more to Him.

Actually, our daily needs are small. It is wonderful how simply we can live. Why then give food and clothing such a prominent place in our lives? And why be of doubtful mind, worrying about the future? This is the way unsaved people live. The nations of the earth who do not know God as their Father concentrate on food, clothing, and pleasure. These things form the very center and circumference of their existence. But God never intended His children should spend their time in the mad rush for creature comforts. He has a work to be done on earth, and has promised to care for those who give themselves wholeheartedly to Him. If we seek His kingdom, He will never let us starve or be naked. How sad it would be to come to the end of life and realize most of our time was spent in slaving for what was already included in the ticket home to heaven.

The disciples formed a little flock of defenseless sheep, sent out into the midst of an unfriendly world. They had no visible means of support or defense. Yet this bedraggled group of young men was destined to inherit the kingdom with Christ. They would one day reign with Him over all the earth. In view of this, the Lord encouraged them not to fear, because if God had such glorious honors in store for them, then they need not worry about the pathway that lay between.

Instead of accumulating material possessions and planning for time, they can put these possessions to work for the Lord. In this way they would be investing for heaven and for eternity. The ravages of age could not affect their possessions. Heavenly treasures are fully insured against theft and spoilage. The trouble with material wealth is that ordinarily you can't have it without trusting it. This is why the Lord Jesus said, "Where your treasure is, there your heart will be also." If we send our money on ahead, then our affections will be weaned from the perishing things of this world.

> **Heavenly treasures are fully insured against theft and spoilage.**

Be Ready! (12:35-40)

Not only were the disciples to trust the Lord for their needs, they were to live in constant expectancy of His coming again. Their "waists" were to be girded and their lamps burning. In eastern lands, a belt was drawn around the waist to hold up the long flowing garments when a person was about to walk quickly or run. The girded waist speaks of a mission to be accomplished and the burning lamp suggests a testimony to be maintained.

The disciples were to live in momentary expectation of the Lord's return, as if He were a man returning from a marriage feast. "They should be free from all earthly encumbrances, so that the moment the Lord knocks, according to the figure, they may open to Him immediately—without distraction or having to get ready. Their hearts are waiting for Him, for their Lord; they love Him, they are waiting for Him. He knocks and they open to Him immediately."[5]

The details of the story concerning the man returning from the wedding feast should not be pressed as far as the prophetic future is concerned. We should not identify the wedding feast here with the marriage supper of the Lamb, or the man's return with the rapture. The Lord's story was designed to teach one simple truth, namely, watchfulness for His return; it was not intended to set forth the order of events at His coming.

When the man comes back from the wedding, his servants are eagerly waiting for him, ready to swing into action at his command. He is so pleased with their watchful attitude that he turns the tables, as it were. He girds himself with a servant's apron, seats them at the table, and serves them a meal. This is a very touching suggestion that He who once came into this world in the form of a bond-slave will graciously condescend to serve His people again in their heavenly home. Bengel regarded this as the greatest promise in the Bible (v. 37).

The second watch of the night was from 9 p.m. to midnight. The third was from midnight to 3 a.m. No matter what watch it was when the lord returned, his servants were waiting for him.

In verses 39 and 40, the Lord Jesus changes the picture. Here He alludes to a homeowner whose house was broken into by thieves. It happened in an unguarded moment. The coming of the thief was entirely unexpected. If the master had known, he would not have allowed his house to be broken into. The lesson is that the time of Christ's coming is uncertain; no one knows the day or the hour when He will appear. When He does come, those believers who had laid up treasures on earth will lose them all, because as someone has said, "A Christian either leaves his wealth or goes to it." If we are really watching for Christ's return, we will sell all that we have and lay up treasures in heaven where no thief can reach them.

Faithful and Unfaithful Servants (12:41-48)

At this point Peter asked if Christ's talk on watchfulness was intended for the disciples alone or for everyone. The Lord answered it was for all who profess to be stewards of God.

——— ❧ ———
People are important, not things.
——— ❧ ———

The wise and faithful steward is the one who is set over the Master's household and who gives food to His people. Notice the steward's main responsibility here concerns people, not material things. This is in keeping with the entire context, warning the disciples against materialism and covetousness. It is people who are important, not things.

When the Lord comes and finds His bond-slave taking a genuine interest in the spiritual welfare of men and women, He will reward him liberally. The reward probably has to do with government rule with Christ during the millennium (1 Peter 5:1-4).

The servant in verse 45 professes to be working for Christ, but actually he is an unbeliever. Instead of feeding the people of God, he abuses them, robs them, and lives in self-indulgence. (This may be a reference to the Pharisees.) The coming of the Lord will expose his unreality, and he will be punished with all other unbelievers. The expression "cut him in two" in verse 46 may also be translated "severely scourge him" (AV Margin).

Verses 47 and 48 set forth a fundamental principle in regard to all service. The principle is that the greater the privilege, the greater the responsibility. For believers, it means there will be degrees of reward in heaven. For unbelievers, it means there will be degrees of punishment in hell.

———— ❧ ————

The greater the privilege, the greater the responsibility.

———— ❧ ————

Those who have come to know God's will as it is revealed in the Scriptures are under great responsibility to obey it. Much has been given to them; much will be required of them. Those who have not been so highly privileged will be punished for their misdeeds, but their punishment will be less severe.

Effects of Christ's First Advent (12:49-53)

The Lord Jesus knew His coming to the earth would not bring peace at the outset. First it must cause division, strife, persecution, bloodshed. He did not come with the avowed purpose of casting this kind of fire on the earth, but that was the result or effect of His coming. Although afflictions and dissentions broke out during His earthly ministry, it was not until the cross that the heart of man was truly exposed. The Lord Jesus knew all of this must take place, and He was willing for the fire of persecution to burst forth as soon as necessary against Himself.

He had a baptism (immersion) to be baptized with—His "immersion" in the "waters" of death on the cross of Calvary. He was under tremendous constraint to go to the cross to accomplish redemption for lost mankind. The shame, suffering, and death were the Father's will for Him, and He was anxious to obey.

Jesus knew very well His coming would not give peace to the earth at that time. And so He warned the disciples that when men came to Him, their families would persecute them and drive them out. The introduction of Christianity into an average home of five would split the family. It is a curious mark of man's perverted nature that ungodly relatives would often rather have their son a drunkard and dissolute person than have him take a public stand as a disciple of the Lord Jesus Christ.

This shows that Jesus did not come to unite all men (godly and ungodly) into a single "universal brotherhood of man" but to divide them as they had never been divided before.

Weather–wise, Time–foolish (12:54-59)

The previous verses were addressed to the disciples. Now the Savior turns to the multitude. He reminds them of their skill in predicting the weather. They knew when they saw a cloud to the west (over the Mediterranean), they were in for some rain. On the other hand, a south wind would bring scorching heat and drought. The people had the intelligence to know this, and the will to know it too.

In spiritual matters, it was a different story. Though they had normal human intelligence, they did not realize the important time that had arrived in human history. The Son of God had come to this earth, and was standing in their very midst. Heaven had never come so near before. But they did not discern it. They had the intellectual capacity to know, but they did not have the will to know, and thus they were self-deluded.

If they realized the significance of the day in which they lived, they would be in a hurry to make peace with their Adversary (vv. 58-59). Four legal terms are used here—adversary, magistrate, judge, officer—and they all may refer to God. At the time God was walking in and out among them, pleading with them, giving them an opportunity to be saved. They should repent and put their faith in Him. If they refused, they would have to stand before God as their Judge. The case would be sure to go against them. They would be found guilty and condemned for their unbelief. They would be cast into prison, that is, eternal punishment. They would not come out till they had paid the last mite—which means they would never come out, because they would never be able to pay such a tremendous debt.

So Jesus was saying they should discern the time in which they lived. Then they should get right with God by repenting of their sins and by committing themselves to Him in full surrender.

[1] H. A. Ironside, *Address on the Gospel of Luke* (New York: Loizeaux Brothers, 1947) p. 390.
[2] William Kelly, *op. cit.*, p. 199.
[3] F. L. Godet, *Commentary on the Gospel of Luke*, Vol. II (Grand Rapids: Zondervan Publishing House, n.d.) p. 89.
[4] Jr. R. Miller, *Come Ye Apart* (New York: Thomas Crowell and Co., 1887) reading for June 10.
[5] William Kelly, *op. cit.*, p. 214.

7

WARNINGS
(13:1–14:35)

"Unless You Repent . . ." (13:1-5)

The previous chapter closed with the failure of the Jewish nation to discern the time in which they lived, and the warning from the Lord Jesus to repent quickly or perish forever. Chapter 13 continues this general subject, and is largely addressed to Israel as a nation, although the principles apply to individual people.

Two national calamities form the basis of the ensuing conversation. The first was the massacre of some Galileans who had come to Jerusalem to worship. Pilate, governor of Judea, had ordered them to be slain while they were offering sacrifices. Little else is known concerning this atrocity. We assume the victims were Jews who had been living in Galilee.

The Jews in Jerusalem might have been laboring under the delusion that these Galileans must have committed terrible sins, and that their death was an evidence of God's disfavor. However, the Lord Jesus corrected this by warning the Jewish people that unless they repented, they would likewise perish.

The other tragedy concerned the collapse of a tower in Siloam that caused the death of eighteen persons. Little or nothing else is known about this accident except what is recorded here. Fortunately, it is not necessary to know any further details. The point emphasized by Jesus was that this catastrophe should not be interpreted as a special judgment for gross wickedness. Rather it should be seen as a warning to all the nation of Israel that a similar doom would come upon them unless they repented. This doom came in AD 70 when Titus invaded Jerusalem.

The Fruitless Fig Tree (13:6-9)

In close connection with the preceding passage, the Lord Jesus told the parable of the fig tree. It is not difficult to identify the fig tree as Israel, planted in God's vineyard, that is, the world. God looked for fruit on the tree, but He found none. So He said to the vinedresser (the Lord Jesus Christ) that He had looked in vain for fruit from the tree for three years. The simplest interpretation of this refers it to the first three years of our Lord's public ministry. The thought of the passage is that the fig tree had been given sufficient time to produce fruit, if it was ever going to do so. If no fruit appeared in three years, then it was reasonable to conclude that none ever would appear. Because of its fruitlessness, God ordered it to be cut down. It was only occupying ground that could be used more productively. The vinedresser interceded for the fig tree, asking it be given one more year. If at the end of that time it was still fruitless, then it would be cut down. This is what happened. It was after the fourth year had begun that Israel rejected and crucified the Lord Jesus. As a result, its capital was destroyed and the people scattered.

"The Son of God knew the mind of His Father, the Owner of the vineyard, and that the dread order 'Cut it down' had been issued; Israel had again exhausted the Divine forbearance. Neither a nation nor a person has reason to enjoy the care of God if not bringing forth the fruits of righteousness unto the glory and praise of God. Man exists for the honor and pleasure of the Creator. When he does not serve this just end why should not the sentence of death follow his sinful failure, and he be removed from his place of privilege?"[1]

Healing Miracle on the Sabbath (13:10-17)

The real attitude of Israel toward the Lord Jesus is seen in the ruler of the synagogue. This official objected that Jesus had healed a woman on the Sabbath day. The woman had suffered from severe curvature of the spine for eighteen years. Her deformity was great; she could not straighten herself up at all. Without even being asked, the Lord Jesus had spoken the healing word, laid His hands upon her, and straightened her spine.

The ruler of the synagogue indignantly told the people they should come for healing on the first six days of the week, but not on the seventh. It is clear he was a professional religionist. He had no deep concern for the problems of the people. Even if they had come on the first six days of the week, he could not have helped them. He was a stickler about the technical points of the law, but there was no love or mercy in his heart. "If that ruler had had curvature of the spine for eighteen years, he would not have minded on which day he was straightened out" (Daily Notes).

Jesus reproved his hypocrisy and that of the other leaders. He reminded them that they didn't hesitate to loose an ox or an ass from the stall on the Sabbath in order to let it drink water. If they showed such consideration for dumb animals on the Sabbath, was it wrong for the Lord Jesus to perform an act of healing on this woman who was a daughter of Abraham? The expression "a daughter of Abraham" indicates not only that she was a Jewess but also a true believer, a woman of faith.

Verse 16 indicates the curvature of the spine was caused by Satan. We know from other portions of the Word that some sicknesses are the result of satanic activity. Job's boils were inflicted by Satan. Paul's thorn in the flesh was a messenger of Satan to buffet him. The devil is not allowed to do this on a believer, however, without the Lord's permission. And God overrules any such sickness or suffering for His own glory.

The critics of our Lord were thoroughly put to shame by His words. The common people rejoiced because a glorious miracle had been performed, and they knew it.

The Parables of the Kingdom (13:18-21)

After seeing this wonderful miracle of healing, the people might have been tempted to think that the kingdom would be set up immediately. Jesus corrected them by setting forth two parables of the kingdom of God that describe it as it would exist between the time of the King's rejection and His return to the earth to reign. They picture the growth of Christendom, and include mere profession as well as reality (see notes on 8:1-3).

First, He likened the kingdom of God to a grain of mustard seed. This is one of the tiniest of the seeds, yet when cast into the ground, it sometimes produces a tree of abnormal growth about the size of a fruit tree. It is big enough for birds of the heaven to lodge in its branches. The thought here is that Christianity had a humble beginning, small as a grain of mustard seed. But as it grew, it became popularized, and Christendom as we know it today developed. Christendom is composed of all who profess allegiance to the Lord, whether or not they have ever been born again. The birds of the heaven are vultures or birds of prey. They are symbols of evil, and picture the fact that Christendom has become the resting place for various forms of corruption.

The second parable likened the kingdom of God to leaven that a woman placed in three measures of meal. Leaven in the Scripture is always a symbol of evil. Here the thought is that evil doctrine has been introduced into the pure food of the people of God. This evil doctrine is not static; it has an insidious power to spread.

Who Will Enter the Kingdom? (13:22-30)

As the Lord Jesus moved on toward Jerusalem, someone stepped out from the crowd to ask Him if only a few would be saved. Actually it was an idle question, provoked by mere curiosity. The Lord Jesus simply warned the questioner to make sure he himself would enter by the straight gate.

When Jesus said to strive to enter by "the narrow gate," He did not mean salvation requires effort on our part. The narrow gate here is new birth—salvation by grace, through faith. Jesus was warning the man to make sure he entered by this door.

> The day of grace in which we live will come to an end.

Many will seek to enter but will not be able when once the door is shut. This does not mean they will seek to enter in by the door of conversion, but in the day of Christ's power and glory, they will want admission to His kingdom, but it will be too late. The day of grace in which we live will come to an end. The master of the house will rise up and shut the door. The Jewish nation is pictured then as knocking at the door and asking the Lord to open. He will refuse on the ground that He never knew them. They will protest, pretending they had lived on very intimate terms with Him. But He will not be moved by these pretensions. They were workers of iniquity, and will not be allowed to enter in. His refusal will cause weeping and gnashing of teeth. The weeping indicates remorse and the gnashing of teeth speaks of violent hatred of God. This shows that the sufferings of hell do not change the heart of man.

Unbelieving Israelites will see Abraham, Isaac, and Jacob, and all the prophets in the kingdom of God. They themselves expected to be there, simply because they were related to Abraham, Isaac, and Jacob, but they will be cast forth outside. Gentiles will travel to the brightness of Christ's kingdom from all corners of the earth and enjoy its wonderful blessings. Thus the Jews who were first in God's plan for blessing will be rejected, while the Gentiles who were looked down upon as dogs will enjoy the blessings of Christ's millennial reign.

Not Galilee, But Jerusalem (13:31-35)

At this time, the Lord Jesus was apparently in Herod's territory. Some of the Pharisees came and warned Him to get out because Herod was trying to kill Him. The Pharisees seem completely out of character in thus professing an interest in Jesus' welfare and safety. Perhaps they had joined in a plot with Herod to frighten Jesus into going to Jerusalem, where He would most certainly be arrested. Herod might not have wanted to kill Jesus, himself, since the murder of John the Baptist was still nagging at his conscience. Jesus was not moved by the threat of physical violence. He recognized in it a plot on Herod's part and told the disciples to go back to that she-fox with a message. Some people have difficulty with the fact that the Lord Jesus spoke of Herod as a she-fox. They feel it was in violation of the Scripture that forbids speaking evil of a ruler of the people (Ex. 22:28). However, this was not evil; it was the absolute truth.

> No power on earth could harm the Lord Jesus until the appointed time.

The gist of the message sent by Jesus was that He still had work to do for a short time. He would cast out demons and perform healing miracles during the few remaining days allotted to Him. Then on the third day, the final day He would have finished the work connected with His earthly ministry. Nothing would hinder Him in the performance of His duties. No power on earth could harm Him until the appointed time. What's more, He could not be slain in Galilee. This prerogative was reserved for the city of Jerusalem. It was Jerusalem that characteristically had murdered the servants of the Most High God. Jerusalem had more or less a monopoly on the death of God's spokesmen. That is what the Lord Jesus meant when He said, "it cannot be that a prophet should perish outside of Jerusalem" (v. 33).

Having thus spoken the truth concerning this wicked city, the Lord Jesus turned in pathos and wept over it. This city that killed the prophets and stoned God's messengers was the object of His tender love. How often

He would have gathered the people of the city together like a hen gathers her brood, but they were not willing. The difficulty lay in their stubborn will. As a result, their city, their temple, and their land would be left desolate. They would pass through a long period of exile. In fact, they would not see the Lord until they changed their attitude toward Him. Verse 35b refers to the second advent of Christ. A remnant of the nation of Israel will repent then and will say, "Blessed is He who comes in the name of the Lord." His people will then be willing in the day of His power.

Jesus Heals a Man on the Sabbath (14:1-6)

One Sabbath day, a ruler of the Pharisees invited the Lord to his house for a meal. It was not a sincere gesture of hospitality, but rather an attempt on the part of the religious leaders to find fault with Jesus. Jesus saw a man standing there who was afflicted with dropsy (swelling caused by the accumulation of water in the tissues). Jesus read the minds of His critics by asking them pointedly whether it was lawful to heal on the Sabbath. Much as they would like to have said it was not, they could not support their answer, and so they remained silent. Jesus therefore healed the man and let him go. To Him it was a work of mercy, and divine love never ceases its activities, even on the Sabbath (John 5:17).

Turning to the Jews, Jesus reminded them that if one of their animals fell into a pit on the Sabbath, they would certainly help the animal out. It was in their own interest to do so. The animal was worth money to them. In the case of a suffering fellow man, they didn't care, and they would have condemned the Lord Jesus for helping him. Although they could not answer Jesus' reasoning, we can be sure that they were all the more angry with Him.

Where to Sit at a Feast (14:7-11)

As the Lord Jesus entered the Pharisee's house, He perhaps had seen the guests maneuvering for the best places around the table. They sought the positions of eminence and honor. The fact He too was a guest did not prevent Him from speaking out in frankness and righteousness. He warned them against this form of self-seeking. When they were invited to a meal, they should take the lower place rather than the higher. When we seek a high place for ourselves, there is always the possible shame of being demoted. If we are truly humble before God, there is only one direction we can possibly move and that is up. Jesus taught that it is better to be advanced to a place of honor than to grasp it and later have to give it up. He Himself is the living example of self-renunciation (Phil. 2:5-8). He humbled Himself and God exalted Him. Those who exalt themselves will be humbled by God.

Whom to Invite to a Supper (14:12-14)

The ruler of the Pharisees had undoubtedly invited the local celebrities to this meal. Jesus perceived this at once. He noticed that the under-privileged people in the community were not included. He therefore took occasion to voice one of the great principles of

——— ✍ ———
We should love those who are unlovely, and cannot repay us.
——— ✍ ———

Christianity: that we should love those who are unlovely, and cannot repay us. The usual way for men to act is to invite their friends, relatives, and rich neighbors, always with the hope of being repaid in kind. It does not require divine life to act in this way. But it is positively *super*natural to show kindness to the poor, the maimed, the lame, and the blind. God reserves a special reward for those who show charity to these classes.

Although such guests will not be able to repay us, yet God Himself promises to reward at the resurrection of the just. This is also known in the Scripture as the first resurrection, and includes the resurrection of all true believers. It takes place at the rapture, and also, we believe, at the end of the tribulation period. The first resurrection is not one single event, but takes place in stages.

The Guests Who Declined (14:15-24)

One of the guests who reclined with Jesus at the meal remarked how wonderful it would be to participate in the blessings of the kingdom of God. Perhaps he was impressed by the principles of conduct that the Lord Jesus had just taught. Or perhaps it was just a general remark which he made without too much thought. The Lord replied that wonderful as it may be to eat bread in the kingdom of God, the sad fact is many of those who are invited make all kinds of foolish excuses for their failure to accept. He pictured God as a certain man who made a great supper and sent out an invitation to many guests. When the meal was ready, he asked his servant to notify the invited guests that everything was now ready. This reminds us of the great fact that the Lord Jesus finished the work of redemption on the cross of Calvary. The gospel invitation goes out on the basis of its completion.

One person who had been invited excused himself because he had bought a field and wanted to go and see it. Normally he should have gone and seen it before purchasing it. But even then, he was putting the love of material things ahead of the gracious invitation. The next one had bought five yoke of oxen, and was going to prove them. He pictures those who put jobs, occupations, or business ahead of the call of God. The third one said he had married a wife, and thus could not come. Family ties and social relationships often hinder men from accepting the gospel invitation.

When the servant notified his master that the invitation was being rejected right and left, the master sent him forth to the city to invite the poor, the maimed, the blind and the lame. "Both nature and grace abhor a vacuum" (Bengel). Perhaps the first ones invited picture the leaders of the Jewish people. When they rejected the gospel, God sent it out to the common people of the city of Jerusalem. Many of these responded to the call, but still there was room in the master's house. And so the lord said to the servant to go out into the highways and by-ways and persuade men to come in. This doubtless pictures the gospel going out to the Gentile people. They were not to be compelled by force of arms (as has been done in the history of the church), but rather by force of argument. Loving persuasion was to be used in an effort to bring them in so that the master's house might be filled. Thus the original guest list was no longer useful when the meal was held because those originally invited did not come.

Terms of Discipleship (14:25-35)

Great multitudes followed the Lord Jesus. Most leaders would be elated by such a widespread interest, but the Lord Jesus was looking for those who were willing to live devotedly and passionately for Him, and even die for Him if necessary. He now began to sift the crowd by presenting to them the stringent terms of discipleship. At times the Lord Jesus wooed men to Himself, but after they began to follow Him, He winnowed them. That is what is taking place here.

First, He told those who followed Him that true disciples must love Him supremely (v. 25). He never suggested men should have bitter hatred in their hearts toward father, mother, wife, children, brothers, and sisters. He was emphasizing that love for Christ must be so great that all other loves are mere pretense by comparison (compare Matthew 10:37). No consideration of family ties must ever be allowed to deflect a disciple from a pathway of full obedience to the Lord.

The most difficult part of this first term of discipleship is found in the words "and his own life also." We must not only love our relatives less; we must hate our own lives also. Instead of living self-centered lives, we must live Christ-centered lives. Instead of asking how every action will affect ourselves, we must be careful to assess how it will affect Christ and His glory. Considerations of personal comfort and safety must be subordinated to the great task of glorifying Christ and making Him known. The Savior's words are absolute. He said if we did not love Him supremely, more than our family and our own lives, we could not be His disciples. There is no half-way measure.

> **Instead of living self-centered lives, we must live Christ-centered lives.**

Second, a true disciple must bear his own cross and follow Him. The cross is not some physical infirmity or mental anguish, but a pathway of reproach, suffering, loneliness, and even death which a person voluntarily chooses for Christ's sake. Not all believers bear the cross. It is possible to avoid it by living a nominal Christian life. But if we determine to be all out for Christ, we will experience the same kind of satanic opposition which the Son of God knew when He was here on earth. This is the cross.

The disciple must come after Christ. He must live the type of life Christ lived when He was here on earth—a life of self-renunciation, humiliation, persecution, reproach, temptation, and contradiction of sinners against Himself.

The Lord Jesus used two illustrations to emphasize the necessity of counting the cost before setting out to follow Him. He likened the Christian life to a building project and to warfare. A man intending to build a tower first sits down and counts the cost. If he doesn't have enough to finish it, he doesn't proceed. Otherwise when the foundation is laid, and the work must stop, the onlookers begin to mock him, saying "This man began to build and was not able to finish." So it is with disciples. They should first count the cost, whether they really mean to abandon their lives wholeheartedly to Christ. Otherwise they might start off in a blaze of glory, and then fizzle out. If so, the onlookers will mock them for beginning well and ending ingloriously. The world has nothing but contempt for half-hearted Christians.

A king going to war against forces numerically superior must consider carefully whether his smaller forces have the capacity to defeat the enemy. He realizes full well it is either absolute committal or abject surrender. And so it is in the life of Christian discipleship. There can be no halfway measures.

Verse 33 is probably one of the most unpopular verses in the entire Bible. It explicitly states, "Whoever of you does not forsake all that he has cannot be My disciple." There is no evading the meaning of the words. They do not say a person must

> The world has nothing but contempt for half-hearted Christians.

be *willing* to forsake all. Rather, they say he must forsake all. We must give the Lord Jesus credit for knowing what He was saying. He realized the job would never be done in any other way. He must have men and women who esteem Him more than everything else in the world.

"The man who does well for himself is the man who gives up everything for Christ's sake. He makes the best of bargains; he carries the cross for a few years in this world, and in the world to come has everlasting life. He obtains the best of possessions; he carries his riches with him beyond the grave. He is rich in grace here, and he is rich in glory hereafter. And, best of all, what he obtains by faith in Christ he never loses. It is 'that good part which is never taken away.'"[2]

In verse 34 salt is a picture of a disciple. There is something wholesome and commendable about a person who is living devotedly and sacrificially for the Lord. But then we read of salt that has lost its savor. Actually, the salt on our table cannot lose its savor because it is pure salt. But in Bible lands, the salt was often mixed with various forms of impurity. Therefore it was possible for salt to be wasted away and for a residue to remain in the container. This residue was worthless. It could not even be used for fertilizing the land. It had to be discarded.

The picture is of a disciple who starts off brilliantly, and then goes back on his vows. The disciple has one basic reason for existence; if he fails, then he is a pitiable object. We read concerning the salt that "men throw it out." It does not say *God* throws it out; this is impossible. But men throw it out by trampling underfoot the testimony of one who began to build and was not able to finish.

"There is shown the danger of what begins well turning out ill. What is there in the world so useless as salt when it has lost the one property for which it is valued? It is worse than useless for any other purpose. So with the disciple who ceases to be Christ's disciple. He is not suited for the world's purposes, and he has forsaken God's. He has too much light or knowledge for entering into the vanities and sins of the world, and he has no enjoyment of grace and truth to keep him in the path of Christ. . . . Savorless salt becomes an object of contempt and judgment."[3]

The Lord Jesus closed the message on discipleship with the words "He who has ears to hear, let him hear!" These words imply not everyone will have the willingness to listen to the stringent terms of discipleship. But if a person is willing to follow the Lord Jesus, no matter what the cost may be, then he should hear and follow.

Calvin once said, "I gave up all for Christ, and what have I found? I have found everything in Christ." Henry Drummond said, "The entrance fee into the kingdom of heaven is nothing: the annual subscription is everything."

[1] G. H. Lang, *op. cit.*, p. 230.
[2] John Charles Ryle, *Expository Thoughts on the Gospels, St. Luke*, Vol. II (New York: Fleming H. Revell Co., 1858) p. 86.
[3] William Kelly, *op. cit.*, p. 249.

8

GROWING OPPOSITION
(15:1–16:31)

Complaint of the Pharisees (15:1-2)

The teaching ministry of our Lord in chapter 14 seemed to attract the despised tax-collectors and others who were outwardly sinners. Although Jesus reproved their sins, yet many of them acknowledged He was right. They took sides with Christ against themselves. In true repentance, they acknowledged Him as Lord. Wherever Jesus found people who were willing to acknowledge their sin, He gravitated toward them, and bestowed spiritual help and blessing upon them.

The scribes and Pharisees resented the fact that Jesus fraternized with people who were avowedly sinners. They did not show grace to these social and moral lepers, and resented Jesus doing so. They hurled a charge at Him, "This Man receives sinners and eats with them." The charge was true. They thought it was blameworthy, but actually it was in fulfillment of the very purpose for which the Son of God came into the world.

Jesus recounted the parable of the lost sheep, the lost coin, and the lost son in answer to their charge. These stories were aimed directly at the scribes and Pharisees who were never broken before God to admit their lost condition. The fact was, they were as lost as the tax-collectors and sinners, but they

> God receives real joy and satisfaction when He sees sinners repenting.

refused to admit it. The point of the three stories is that God receives real joy and satisfaction when He sees sinners repenting, whereas He obtains no gratification from self-righteous hypocrites who are too proud to admit their sinful wretchedness.

The Lost Sheep (15:3-7)

Here the Lord Jesus is pictured under the symbol of a shepherd. The ninety-nine sheep represent the scribes and Pharisees. The lost sheep typifies a tax-collector or an acknowledged sinner. When the Shepherd realizes one of His sheep is lost, He leaves the ninety-nine in the wilderness (not in the fold) and goes out after it until He finds it. As far as our Lord was concerned, this journey included His descent to earth, His years of public ministry, His rejection, suffering, and death.

Having found the sheep, He laid it on His shoulders and took it to His home. The saved sheep enjoyed a place of privilege and intimacy it never knew as long as it was numbered with the others. The Shepherd summoned His neighbors to rejoice with Him over the salvation of the lost sheep. This speaks of the Savior's joy in seeing a sinner repent.

The lesson drawn from the story is clear. There is joy in heaven over one sinner who repents, but there is no joy over the ninety-nine sinners who have never been convicted of their lost condition. Verse 7 does not actually mean there are some persons who need no repentance. All men are sinners, and all must repent in order to be saved. The verse describes those who, as far as they see themselves, need no repentance.

The Lost Coin (15:8-10)

The woman in this story may represent the Holy Spirit, seeking the lost with the lamp of the Word of God. The nine pieces of silver speak of the unrepentant, whereas the lost coin suggests the man who is willing to confess he is out of touch with God. In the previous account the sheep wandered away by its own choice. Here, the coin is an inanimate object and might suggest the lifeless condition of the sinner. He is dead in trespasses and in sin.

The woman continued to search for the coin until she found it. Then she called her neighbors to celebrate with her. The lost coin that she had found brought her more true pleasure than the nine that had never been lost. So it is with God. The sinner who humbles himself and confesses his lost condition brings joy to the heart of God. He obtains no such joy from those who never feel their need for repentance.

The Prodigal Son (15:11-32)

God the Father is depicted here as a certain man who had two sons. The younger son typifies the repentant sinner, whereas the elder son illustrates the scribes and the Pharisees. The latter are sons of God by creation but not redemption.

The younger son is also known as the prodigal son. A prodigal is one who is recklessly extravagant, spending money wastefully. This son became weary of his father's house and decided he wanted to leave. He could not wait for his father to die, and so asked for his portion of the inheritance ahead of time. The father distributed to his sons their proper share. Shortly afterward, the younger son set out to a distant land and spent his money freely in sinful pleasures. As soon as his funds were gone a severe depression gripped the land, and he found himself destitute. The only employment he could get was as a feeder of swine—a job that would have been most distasteful to the average Jew. As he watched the pigs eating their bean pods, he envied them. They had more to eat than he had, and no one seemed disposed to help him. The friends he had when he was spending money freely had all disappeared.

The famine proved to be a blessing in disguise. It made him think. He remembered his father's hired servants were living far more comfortably than he. They had plenty of food to eat, while he was wasting away with hunger. As he thought of this, he decided to do something about it. He determined to go back to his father in repentance, acknowledge his sin, and seek pardon. He realized he was no more worthy to be called his father's son, and planned to ask for a job as a hired servant (Luke 15:19).

Long before he reached his home, the father saw him and rushed out to meet him. He ran and fell on his neck and kissed him. This is probably the only time in the Bible where haste is used of God in a good sense.

"Daringly Jesus pictured God, not waiting for His shamed child to slink home, nor standing on his dignity when he came, but running out to gather him, shamed and ragged and muddied as he was, to his welcoming arms. The same name 'Father' has at once darkened the color of sin and heightened the splendid glory of forgiveness."[1]

The son made his confession up to the point where he was going to ask for employment. But the father interrupted by ordering the slaves to put the best robe on his son, a ring on his hand, and shoes on his feet. He also ordered a great feast to celebrate the return of his son who had been lost and was now found. As far as the father was concerned, he had been dead but now was alive again. "The young man was looking for a good time, but he did not find it in the far country. He found it only when he had the good sense to come back to his father's house." It has often been pointed out that "they began to be merry" but it is never recorded that their joy ended. So it is with the salvation of the sinner.

When the elder son returned from the field and heard all the merry-making, he asked the servants what was going on. They told him his younger brother had returned home and his father was delirious with joy. The elder son was consumed with a jealous rage. He refused to participate in his father's joy. "Where God's happiness is, there self-righteousness cannot come. If God is good to the sinner, what avails my righteousness?" (J. N. Darby).

When his father urged him to participate in the festivities, he refused, moaning that the father had never rewarded him for his faithful service and obedience. He had never been given a kid, to say nothing of a fatted calf. He complained that when the prodigal son returned, after spending his father's money on harlots, the father did not hesitate to make a great feast. Note, in verse 30, he said "this son of yours," not "this my brother."

The father's answer indicated there is a joy connected with the restoration of a lost one, whereas an obstinate, ungrateful, unreconciled son produces no cause for celebration.

The elder son is an eloquent picture of the scribes and Pharisees. They resented God's showing mercy to outrageous sinners. To their own way of thinking, if not to God's, they had served Him faithfully, had never transgressed His commandments, and yet had never been properly rewarded for all of this. The truth was that they were religious hypocrites and guilty sinners. Their pride blinded them to their distance from God, and to the fact that He had lavished blessing after blessing upon them. If they had only been willing to repent and to acknowledge their sins, then the Father's heart would have been gladdened and they too would have been the cause of great celebration.

The Unjust Steward (16:1-13)

The Lord Jesus now turns from the Pharisees and scribes to His disciples with a lesson on stewardship. This paragraph is admittedly one of the most difficult in the gospel. The reason for the difficulty is that the story of the unjust steward seems to commend dishonesty. In fact, it seems that the Lord Himself praises the steward for his crookedness. We shall see that this is not the case, however, as we proceed.

The wealthy man in this story is a picture of God Himself. A steward is one who is entrusted with the management of another person's property. As far as this story is concerned, any disciple of the Lord is also a steward. This particular steward was accused of embezzling his employer's funds. He was called to account, and notified that he was being dismissed.

> **Any disciple of the Lord is also a steward.**

The steward did some fast thinking. He realized that he must provide for his future. Yet he was too old to engage in hard physical labor, and he was too proud to beg (though not too proud to steal). How then could he provide for his social security? He hit upon a scheme by which he could win friends who would show kindness to him when he was in need. The scheme was this. He went to one of his employer's customers and asked how much he owed. When the customer said 100 measures of oil, the steward told him to pay for 50 measures and the account would be considered closed. Another customer owed 100 measures of wheat. The steward told him to pay for 80 measures, and he would mark the invoice "Paid."

The shocking part of the story is found in verse 8 where the master commended the unjust steward for acting wisely. The Authorized Version is misleading in using the term "the lord," as some think this is referring to the Lord Jesus. It was not the Lord Jesus who commended him, but his own employer. But even that change does not remove the difficulty. The question still remains why anyone should approve of such dishonesty. What the steward did was obviously unjust.

The following verses show that the steward was not at all commended for his crookedness, but rather for his foresight. He had acted prudently. He looked to the future, and made provision for it. He sacrificed present gain for future reward. In applying this to our own lives, we must be very clear on this point, however; the future of the child of God is not on this earth but in heaven. Just as the steward took steps to insure that he would have friends during his retirement here below, so the Christian should use his Master's goods in such a way as to insure a welcoming party when he gets to heaven.

Jesus said that the sons of this world are *for their own generation* wiser than the sons of light. This means that ungodly, unregenerate men show more wisdom in providing for their future in this world than true believers show in laying up treasures in heaven. We should make friends to ourselves *by means of* the mammon of unrighteousness. That is, we should use money and other material things in such a way as to win souls for Christ and thus form friendships that will endure throughout eternity.

As A. T. Pierson says, "Money can be used to buy Bibles, books, tracts and thus, indirectly, the souls of men. Thus what was material and temporal becomes immortal, becomes non-material, spiritual and eternal. Here is a man who has $100. He may spend

> **We should use money to win souls for Christ.**

it all on a banquet or an evening party, in which case the next day there is nothing to show for it. On the other hand, he invests in Bibles at $1 each. It buys a hundred copies of the Word of God. These he judiciously sows as seed of the kingdom, and that seed springs up into a harvest, not of Bibles but of souls. Out of the unrighteous, he has made immortal friends, who when he fails, receive him into everlasting habitations."

This then is the teaching of our Lord. By the wise investment of material possessions, we can have part in the eternal blessing of men and women. We can make sure that when we arrive at the gates of heaven, there will be a welcoming committee of those who were saved through our sacrificial giving and prayers. These people will thank us saying, "It was you who invited me here."

J. N. Darby comments: "Man generally is God's steward; and in another sense and in another way Israel was God's steward, put into God's vineyard, and entrusted with law, promises, covenants, worship. But in all, Israel was found to have wasted His goods. Man looked at as a steward has been found to be entirely unfaithful. Now, what is to be done? God appears, and in the sovereignty of His grace turns that which man has abused on the earth into a means of heavenly fruit. The things of this world being in the hands of man, he is not to be using them for the present enjoyment of this world, which is altogether apart from God, but with a view to the future. We are not to seek to possess the things now, but by the right use of these things to make a provision for other times. It is better to turn all into a friend for another day than to have money now. Man here is gone to destruction. Therefore now, man is a steward out of place."[2]

If we are faithful in our stewardship of that which is a very little (money), then we will be faithful in handling that which is much (spiritual treasures). On the other hand, a man who is unrighteous in using the money that God has entrusted to him is unrighteous when bigger considerations are at stake. The relative unimportance of money is emphasized by the expression "in what is least" (v. 10).

A person who is dishonest in using unrighteous mammon for the Lord can hardly expect Him to entrust true riches to him. Money is called unrighteous mammon. It is not inherently evil in itself. But there probably wouldn't be any need for money if sin had not come into the world. And money is "unrighteous" in that it is characteristically used for purposes other than God's glory. It is contrasted here with true riches. The value of money is uncertain and temporary; the value of spiritual realities is fixed and eternal.

Verse 12 distinguishes between that which is another's and that which is your own. As already mentioned, all that we have—our money, our time, our talents—belong to the Lord, and we are to use them for Him. That which is our own refers to rewards we reap in this life and in the life to come as a result of our faithful service for Christ. If we have not been faithful in that which is His, how can He give us that which is our own?

It is impossible to live for *things* and for God at the same time (v. 13). If we are mastered by money, then we cannot truly be serving the Lord. In order to accumulate wealth, one must devote his finest efforts to the task. In the very act of doing this he robs God of that which is rightfully His. It is a

> If we are mastered by money, then we cannot truly be serving the Lord.

matter of divided loyalty. Motives are mixed. Decisions are not impartial. Where our treasure is, there our heart is also. In the effort to gain wealth, we are serving mammon. It is quite impossible to serve God at the same time. Mammon cries out for all that we have and are—our evenings, our weekends, the time we should be giving to the Lord.

The Covetous Pharisees (16:14-18)

The Pharisees were not only proud and hypocritical; they were covetous as well. They thought that godliness was a way of gain. They chose it as one would choose a lucrative profession. Their service was not intended to glorify God and help their neighbors, but rather to enrich themselves. As they heard Jesus teach that they should forego wealth in this world and lay up their treasures in heaven, they sneered at Him. To them, money was more real than the promises of God. Nothing would hinder them from hoarding wealth.

Outwardly the Pharisees appeared to be pious and spiritual. They reckoned themselves to be righteous in the sight of men. But beneath this deceptive exterior, God saw the greed of their hearts. He was not deceived by their pretensions. The type of life that they displayed and was approved by others (Psalm 49:18) was an abomination in God's sight. They esteemed themselves successful because they combined a religious profession with financial affluence. But as far as God was concerned, they were spiritual adulterers. They professed love for Jehovah, but actually mammon was their god.

The continuity of verses 16-18 is difficult. On first reading, they seem to be quite unrelated to what has gone before, and to what follows. However, we feel they can be best understood by remembering that the subject of this chapter is the covetousness and unfaithfulness of the Pharisees. The very ones who prided themselves on the careful observance of the law are exposed as greedy hypocrites. The spirit of the law is in sharp contrast to the spirit of the Pharisees.

The law and the prophets were in force until John. With these words, Jesus described the legal dispensation that began with Moses and ended with John the Baptist. But now a new dispensation was being inaugurated. From the time of John, the gospel of the kingdom of God was being preached. The Baptist went forth announcing the arrival of Israel's rightful King. He told the people that if they would repent, the Lord Jesus would reign over them. As a result of his preaching and the later preaching of the Lord Himself and of the disciples, there was an eager response on the part of many.

"Everyone is pressing into it." Those who did respond to the message literally stormed into the kingdom. The tax-collectors and sinners, for instance, had to leap over the roadblocks set up by the Pharisees. Others had to deal violently with the love of money in their own hearts. Prejudices had to be overcome. But the new dispensation did not mean that basic moral truths were being discarded. It would be easier for heaven and earth to pass away than for one tittle of the law to fall. A tittle of the law could be compared to the crossing of a "t" or the dotting of an "i."

The Pharisees would like to have thought that they were in the kingdom of God, but the Lord was saying in effect, "You cannot disregard the great moral laws of God and still claim a place in the kingdom." Perhaps they would ask, "What great moral precept are we disregarding?" The Lord then pointed them to the law of marriage. Any man who puts away his wife and marries another commits adultery. And whoever marries a divorced woman commits adultery also. This is exactly what the Pharisees were doing spiritually. The Jewish people were brought into a covenant position with God. But these Pharisees were now turning their backs on God in a mad quest for material wealth. And perhaps the verse suggests that they were guilty of literal adultery as well as spiritual.

The Rich Man and Lazarus (16:19-31)

The Lord concludes His discourse on stewardship of material things by this account of two lives, two deaths, and two hereafters. It should be noted that this is not spoken of as a parable. We mention this because some critics seem to explain away the solemn implications of the story by waving it off as a parable.

At the outset, it should be made clear that the unnamed rich man was not condemned to Hades because of his wealth. The basis of salvation is faith in the Lord, and men are condemned for refusing to believe on Him. But this particular rich man showed that he did not have true saving faith by his careless disregard of the poor man who lay at his gate. If he had had the love of Christ in him, he could not have lived in luxury, comfort, and ease when a fellow human being was outside his front door, begging for a few crumbs of bread. He would have entered violently into the kingdom by abandoning his love of money. It is likewise true that Lazarus was not saved because he was poor. He had trusted the Lord for the salvation of his soul.

Now notice the portrait of the rich man, sometimes called Dives (meaning "rich"). He wore only the most expensive, custom-made clothing, and his table was filled with the choicest, gourmet foods. He lived for self, catering to bodily pleasures and appetites. He had no genuine love for God, and no care for his fellow man. Lazarus presents a striking contrast. He was a wretched beggar, dropped off every day in front of the rich man's house, covered with sores, emaciated with hunger, and plagued by dogs that came to lick his wounds.

When Lazarus died, he was carried by the angels into Abraham's bosom. Many question whether angels actually participate in conveying the souls of believers to heaven. We see no reason, however, for doubting the plain force of the words. Angels minister to believers in this life, and there seems no reason why they should not do so at the time of death. Abraham's bosom is a symbolic expression to denote the place of bliss. To any Jew, the thought of enjoying fellowship with Abraham would suggest inexpressible bliss. We take it that Abraham's bosom is the same as heaven.

> Angels minister to believers in this life, and there seems no reason why they should not do so at the time of death.

When the rich man died, his body was placed in the grave—the body that he had catered to, and for which he had spent so much. But that was not all. His soul, or conscious self, went to Hades. (The word "hell" here in the Authorized Version should be translated "Hades." Hell is the final abode of the wicked dead, and is the same as the lake of fire.) Hades denotes the place of departed spirits. In the Old Testament period, it was spoken of as the abode of both saved and unsaved. Here it is spoken of as the abode of the unsaved, because we read that the rich man was in torment.

It must have come as a shock to the disciples when Jesus said that this rich Jew went to Hades. They had always been taught from the Old Testament that riches were a sign of God's blessing and favor. An Israelite who obeyed the Lord was promised material prosperity. How then could a wealthy Jew go to Hades? The Lord Jesus had just announced that a new order of things began with the preaching of John. Henceforth riches are not a sign of blessing. They are a test of a man's faithfulness in stewardship. To whom much is given, of him will much be required.

Verse 23 disproves the idea of soul sleep, that is, that the soul is not conscious between death and resurrection. It proves that there is conscious existence beyond the grave. In fact, we are struck by the extent of knowledge that the rich man had. He saw Abraham afar off, and Lazarus in his bosom. He was even able to communicate with Abraham. Calling him "Father Abraham," he begged for mercy, pleading that Lazarus might bring a drop of water to cool his tongue. There is, of course, a question as to how a disembodied soul can experience thirst and anguish from flame. We can only conclude that the language is figurative, but that does not mean that the suffering was not real.

Abraham addressed him as "son," meaning that he was a descendant physically, though obviously not spiritually. The patriarch reminded him of his lifetime of luxury, ease, and indulgence. He also rehearsed the poverty and suffering of Lazarus. Now, beyond the grave, the tables were turned. The inequalities of earth were reversed. We learn here that the choices of this life determine our eternal destiny, and once death has taken place, that destiny is fixed (v. 26). There is no passage from the abode of the saved to that of the damned, or vice versa.

———— ❧ ————

The choices of this life determine our eternal destiny.

———— ❦ ————

In death, the rich man suddenly became evangelistic. He wanted someone to go to his five brothers and warn them against coming to this place of torment. Abraham's reply was that these five brothers, being Jews, had the Old Testament Scriptures, and these should be enough to warn them. The rich man contradicted Abraham, stating that if one should go to them from the dead, they would surely believe. However, Abraham had the last word. He stated that failure to listen to the Word of God is final. If people won't heed the Bible, they won't believe if a person rises from the dead. This is conclusively proved in the case of the Lord Jesus Himself. He arose from the dead, and men still do not believe.

From the New Testament Scriptures, we know that when a believer dies, his body goes to the grave, but his soul goes to be with Christ in heaven (2 Cor. 5:8; Phil. 1:23). When an unbeliever dies, his body likewise goes to the grave, but his soul goes to Hades. For him, Hades is a place of suffering and remorse.

At the time of the rapture, the bodies of believers will be raised from the grave and reunited with the spirits and souls (1 Thess. 4:13-18). They will then dwell with Christ eternally. At the judgment of the great white throne, the bodies, spirits, and souls of unbelievers will be reunited (Rev. 20:12-13). They will then be cast into the lake of fire, a place of eternal punishment.

And so chapter 16 closes with a most solemn warning to the Pharisees, and to all who would live for money. They do so at the peril of their souls. As someone has said, "It is better to beg bread on earth than to beg water in hell."

---

[1] James S. Stewart, *op. cit.*, pp. 77, 78.

[2] J. N. Darby, *The Man of Sorrows* (Glasgow: Pickering and Inglish, n.d.) p. 178.

9

ATTITUDES
(17:1–18:43)

The Peril of Offending (17:1-2)

A lmost all commentators mention that the continuity or flow of thought in this chapter is very obscure. It almost seems as if the Lord pieces together several disconnected subjects. However, His opening remarks on the peril of offending may be linked with the story of the rich man at the close of chapter 16. To live in luxury, complacency, and ease could very well prove to be a stumbling block to others, especially to those who are young in the faith. If a man has the reputation of being a Christian, his example will be followed by others. How serious it is, therefore, to lead promising followers of the Lord Jesus Christ into lives of materialism and the worship of "mammon" (money)!

Of course, the principle applies in a very general way. "Little ones" can be stumbled by being encouraged in worldliness. They can be stumbled by being involved in sexual sin. They can be stumbled by any teaching that waters down the plain meaning of the Scriptures. Anything that leads them away from a pathway of simple faith, of devotedness and of holiness is a stumbling block.

Knowing human nature and conditions in the world, Jesus said that it was inevitable that offenses should come. But this does not diminish the guilt of those who cause the offenses. It would be better for such that a millstone was hanged around their neck and were drowned. It seems clear that language as strong as this is intended to picture not only physical death but eternal condemnation as well. When Jesus speaks of stumbling one of these little ones, He probably included more than children. The reference seems to be to disciples who are young in the faith.

The Need for a Forgiving Spirit (17:3-4)

In the Christian life there is not only the peril of stumbling others. There is also the danger of harboring grudges, of refusing to forgive when an offending person apologizes. That is what the Lord deals with in verses 3 and 4.

According to the New Testament, if a Christian is wronged by another Christian, he should first of all forgive the offender in his heart (Ephesians 4:32). This keeps his own soul free from resentment and malice. Then he should go to the offender privately and rebuke him (v. 3; also Matt. 18:15). If he repents, then he should be told that he is forgiven. Even if he sins repeatedly, then says that he repents, he should be forgiven (v. 4). If a private rebuke does not prove effective, then the person who has been wronged should take one or two witnesses (Matt. 18:16). If he will not listen to these, then the matter should be taken before the church. Failure to hear the church should result in excommunication (Matt. 18:17).

The purpose of rebukes and other disciplinary action is not to get even or to humiliate the offender, but to restore him to fellowship with the Lord and with his brothers. All rebukes should be delivered in a spirit of love. We have no way of judging

> All rebukes should be delivered in a spirit of love.

whether an offender's repentance is genuine. We must accept his own word that he has repented. That is why the Lord Jesus says: ". . . if he sins against you seven times in a day, and seven times in a day returns to you, *saying,* 'I repent,' you shall forgive him."

This is the gracious way our Father treats us. No matter how often we fail Him, we still have the assurance that "if we confess our sins, He is faithful and just to forgive us our sins and to cleanse us from all unrighteousness" (1 John 1:9).

Faith (17:5-6)

The thought of forgiving seven times in a single day presented a difficulty, if not an impossibility to the disciples. They felt they did not possess enough grace to do that, so they asked the Lord to increase their faith. The reply of the Lord Jesus indicated that it was not so much a matter of the quantity of faith but of its quality. Also it was not a question of getting more faith but of using the faith they had.

It is our own pride and self-importance that prevent us from forgiving our brothers. That pride needs to be rooted up and cast out. If faith the size of a mustard seed can root up a mulberry tree and plant it in the sea, it can more easily give us victory over the hardness of heart which keeps us from forgiving a brother indefinitely.

The Unprofitable Slave (17:7-10)

The true bond-slave of Christ has no reason for pride. Self-importance must be plucked out by the roots and in its place planted a true sense of unworthiness. This is the lesson we find in the story of the bond-slave. This slave has been plowing or tending the sheep all day. When he comes in from the field at the end of a day of hard work, the master does not tell him to sit down for supper. Rather, he orders him to put on his apron and serve supper. Only after that is done is the slave allowed to eat his own meal. The master does not thank him for doing these things. It is expected of a slave. After all, a slave belongs to his master, and his primary duty is to obey.

So disciples are bond-slaves of the Lord Jesus Christ. They belong to Him, spirit, soul, and body. In the light of Calvary, nothing they can ever do for the Savior is sufficient to pay Him back for what He has done. So after the disciple has done everything that he has been commanded in the New Testament, he must still admit that he is an unprofitable servant who has only done what was his duty to do.

"There are five marks of the bondservant: (1) He must be willing to have one thing on top of another put upon him, without any consideration being given him. (2) In doing this, he must be willing not to be thanked for it. (3) Having done all this, he must not charge the master with selfishness. (4) He must confess that he is an unprofitable servant. (5) He must admit that doing and bearing what he has in the way of meekness and humility, he has not done one stitch more than it was his duty to do."[1]

> The sin of ingratitude is a peril in the life of the disciple.

Where Are the Nine? (17:11-19)

The sin of ingratitude is another peril in the life of the disciple. This is illustrated in the story of the ten lepers. We read that the Lord Jesus was traveling toward Jerusalem along the borders of Samaria and Galilee. It is almost impossible to trace the exact route. Ordinarily He would have passed through Galilee before coming to Samaria. But it is possible that He was here following the border between Samaria and Galilee east to the Jordan River, then south to Jericho on the east side of the Jordan.

As He was drawing near to a certain village, ten lepers saw Him. Because of their diseased condition, they did not come near to Him, but they did cry out from a distance, pleading for Him to heal them, He rewarded their faith by telling them to go and show themselves to the priest. Now this meant that when they reached the priest, they would have been healed from their leprosy. The priest had no power to heal them, but he was designated as the one to pronounce them clean. Obedient to the word of the Lord, the lepers started out toward the priest's dwelling, and as they went they were miraculously healed of the disease.

They all had faith to be healed, but only one out of the ten turned back to thank the Lord. This one, interestingly enough, was a Samaritan, one of the despised neighbors of the Jewish people with whom they had no dealings, He fell on his face—the true posture of worship—and at the feet of Jesus—the true place of worship.

The Lord Jesus plaintively asked if it were not true that ten had been healed, but that only one ("this foreigner," v. 18) had returned to give thanks. What about the other nine? None of them came back to give glory to God. Turning to the Samaritan, the Lord Jesus said, "Arise, go your way. Your faith has made you well."

It has been well said, "Only the grateful 10 percent inherit the true riches of Christ. Christ meets our turning back (v. 15) and our giving of thanks (v. 16) with fresh blessings. 'Your faith has made you well' (v. 19), can mean only one thing. The nine were healed of leprosy. The tenth was saved from sin as well."

The Coming of the Kingdom (17:20-37)

It is difficult to know whether the Pharisees were sincere in the question about the kingdom, or whether they were mocking. But we do know that, as Jews, they entertained hopes of a kingdom that would be brought in with great power and glory. They looked for outward signs and great political upheavals. The Savior told them that the kingdom of God does not come as a result of people watching for it. G. Campbell Morgan said that observation always means the watching of hostility. Whether or not this is so, it seems clear that the Lord Jesus was saying that the kingdom of God, in its present form at least, did not come with outward show. It was not a visible, earthly, temporal kingdom which could be pointed out as being here or there. Rather, the Savior said, the kingdom of God was within them, or better, among them.

The Lord Jesus could not have meant that the kingdom was actually within the hearts of the Pharisees, because these hardened religious hypocrites had no room in their hearts for Christ the King. But He meant that the kingdom of God was in their midst. He was the rightful King of Israel and had performed His miracles, and presented His credentials for all to see. But the Pharisees had no desire to receive Him. And so for them, the kingdom of God had presented itself and was completely unnoticed by them.

Speaking to the Pharisees, the Lord Jesus described the kingdom as something that had already come. When He turned to the disciples, He spoke about the kingdom as a future event that would be set up at His second coming. But first He described the period that would intervene between His first and second advents. The days would come when the disciples would long to see one of the days of the Son of Man, but would not see it. In other words, they would long for one of the days when He was with them on earth and when they enjoyed sweet fellowship with Him. Those days were, in a sense, foretastes of the time when He would return in power and great glory.

Many false messiahs would arise, and rulers would announce that the Messiah had come. But they were not to be deceived by any such false alarms. Christ's second advent would be as visible and unmistakable as the lightning that streaks across the sky. Again, the Lord Jesus told the disciples that before any of this could come to pass He Himself would suffer many things and be rejected by that generation.

Turning back to the subject of His coming to reign, the Lord taught that the days immediately preceding that glorious event would be like the days of Noah. Men ate, drank, and married. These things are not wrong in themselves; they are normal, legitimate human activities. The evil was that men lived for these things and had no thought or time for God. After Noah and his family entered into the ark, the flood came and destroyed the rest of the population. So the second coming of Christ will mean judgment for those who reject His offer of mercy.

Again, the Lord Jesus said that the days preceding His second advent would be similar to those of Lot. Civilization had advanced somewhat by that time; men not only ate and drank, but they bought, they sold, they planted, they built. It was man's effort to bring in a golden era of peace and prosperity without God. In the very day that Lot and his wife and daughters went out from Sodom, fire and brimstone fell from heaven and destroyed the wicked city. And thus it will be in the day that the Son of Man is revealed. Those who concentrate on pleasure, self-gratification, and commerce will be destroyed.

It will be a day when attachment to earthly things will imperil a man's life. If he is on the rooftop, he shouldn't try to salvage any possessions from his house. If he is out in the field, he shouldn't return to his house. He should flee from those places where judgment is about to fall. Although Lot's wife was taken almost by physical force out of Sodom, yet her heart remained in the city. This was indicated by the fact that she turned back. She was out of Sodom, but Sodom was not out of her. As a result God destroyed her by turning her into a pillar of salt. Those who seek to save their lives by caring only for their physical safety, but not caring for their souls, will lose them. On the other hand, any who lose their lives during this period of tribulation because of faithfulness to the Lord will actually be preserving their lives for all eternity.

The coming of the Lord will be a time of separation. Two men will be sleeping together on a bed. One will be taken away in judgment. The other, a believer, will be spared to enter Christ's kingdom. Two women will be grinding together; the one, an unbeliever, will be taken away in the storm of God's wrath; the other, a child of God, will be spared to enjoy millennial blessings with Christ.

─────── ❧ ───────

The coming of the Lord will be a time of separation.

─────── ❧ ───────

Incidentally, verses 34 and 35 contain a veiled hint as to the rotundity of the earth. The fact that it will be night in one part of the earth and day in another, as indicated by the activities mentioned, displays scientific accuracy that was not brought forth by scientists till many years later.

The disciples fully understood from the Savior's words that His second advent would be catastrophic judgment from heaven on an apostate world. So they asked the Lord where this judgment would fall. His answer was that "Wherever the body is, there the eagles will be gathered together."

The "body" here represents all unbelievers, both Jewish and Gentile. The eagles or vultures symbolize impending judgments. The answer therefore is that judgments would swoop down on every form of unbelief and rebellion against God, no matter where found.

The Certainty that God Will Avenge His Elect (18:1-8)

In chapter 17 the Lord Jesus had warned the disciples that afflictions and persecutions lay ahead. Before the time of His glorious appearing, they would be required to go through deep trials. By way of preparation, He gives further instruction concerning prayer. In the following verses we find a praying widow, a praying Pharisee, a praying tax-collector, and a praying beggar.

The parable of the praying widow teaches that men ought always to pray and not to lose heart. This is true in a general sense of all people, and of all kinds of prayer. But the special sense in which it is used here is prayer for God's deliverance in times of testing. "It is prayer without losing heart (fainting), during the long weary interval between the first and second advents."

The parable pictures an unrighteous judge who was usually quite unmoved by fear of God or regard for his fellowmen. There was also a widow who was being oppressed by some unnamed adversary. This widow came to the judge persistently, asking him for justice. She was not really asking for vengeance against her adversary, but rather that she might be delivered from his inhumane treatment. The judge was unmoved by the validity of her case; the fact that she was being treated unjustly did not move him to action in her behalf. However, the *regularity* with which she came before him prompted him to act. Her persistence brought a decision in her favor.

The Lord Jesus explained to the disciples that if an unrighteous judge would act in behalf of a poor widow because of her persistence, how much more will the righteous God intervene in behalf of His elect. The elect here might refer in a special sense to the Jewish remnant during the tribulation period, but it is also true of all oppressed believers in every age. The reason why God has not intervened long ago is because He is longsuffering with human beings, not willing that any should perish. But the day is coming when His spirit will no longer strive with mankind, and then He will punish those who persecute His followers.

The Lord Jesus closed the parable with the question, "When the Son of Man comes, will He really find faith on the earth?" This probably means the kind of faith that the poor widow had. But it may also indicate that when the Lord returns, there will only be a remnant who are true to Him. In the meantime, each of us should be stimulated to the kind of faith that cries night and day to God.

The Pharisee and the Tax-Collector (18:9-14)

The next parable is addressed to people who pride themselves on being righteous, and who despise all others as highly inferior. By labeling the first man as a Pharisee, the Savior did not leave any doubt as to the particular class of people whom He was addressing. Although the Pharisee went through the motions of prayer, he was really not speaking to God. He was rather boasting of his own moral and religious attainments. Instead of comparing himself with God's perfect standard and seeing how sinful he really was, he compared himself with others in the community and prided himself on being better. His frequent repetition of the personal pronoun "I" reveals the true state of his heart as conceited and self-sufficient.

The tax-collector was a striking contrast. Standing before God, he sensed his own utter unworthiness. He was humbled to the dust. He would not so much as lift his eyes to heaven, but beat his breast and cried to God for mercy. "God, be merciful to me a sinner." The margin of the American Standard Version translates it "*the* sinner." He did not think of himself as one sinner among many, but as the sinner who was unworthy of anything from God.

> God exalts the humble, but He humbles those who exalt themselves.

The Lord Jesus reminded His hearers that it is this spirit of self-humiliation and repentance that is acceptable to God. Contrary to what human appearances might indicate, it was the tax-collector who went down to his house justified (in right standing with God). God exalts the humble, but He humbles those who exalt themselves.

Children Brought to Jesus (18:15-17)

This incident reinforces what we have just had before us, namely, that the humility of a little child is necessary for entrance into the kingdom of

God. Mothers crowded around the Lord Jesus with their babies in order that they might receive blessing from Him. The disciples were annoyed by this intrusion into Jesus' time. But Jesus rebuked the disciples, and tenderly called the little children to Him, saying, "Of such is the kingdom of God." Little children need not become adults in order to be saved, but adults do need the simple faith and humility characteristic of a little child in order to enter God's kingdom.

Children can be saved at a very tender age. That age probably varies in the case of individual children, but the fact remains that any child—no matter how young—who wishes to come to Jesus should be permitted to do so, and encouraged in his faith.

Verse 16 answers the question, "What happens to little children when they die?" The answer is that they go to heaven. Jesus clearly said, "Of such is the kingdom of God."

The Power of Riches to Exclude from the Kingdom (18:18-30)

This next section illustrates the case of a person who does *not* receive the kingdom of God as a little child. One day a ruler came to the Lord Jesus, addressing Him as "Good Teacher," and asking what he must do in order to inherit eternal life. The Savior first of all questioned him on the use of the title "good Teacher." Jesus reminded him that only God is good. Our Lord was not denying that He was God, but He was trying to lead the ruler to confess that fact. If Jesus was good, then He must be God, since only God is essentially good.

> Eternal life is not inherited, and is not gained by doing good works.

Then the Lord Jesus dealt with the question, what must I do to inherit eternal life? We know, of course, that eternal life is not inherited, and is not gained by doing good works. Eternal life is the gift of God through Jesus Christ. In taking the ruler back to the Ten Commandments, Jesus was not implying that he could ever be saved by keeping the law. Rather He was using the law in an effort to convict the man of sin. The Lord Jesus recited the five commandments that have to do with our duty to our fellow men, the second table (tablet) of the law.

It is clear that the law did not have its convicting effect in the life of the man, because he claimed to have kept these commandments from his youth up. Jesus told him that he lacked one thing: love for his neighbor. If he had really kept these commandments, then he would have sold all his possessions and distributed them to the poor. But the fact of the matter was that he did not love his neighbor as himself. He was living a selfish life, with no real love for others. This is proved by the fact that when he heard these things, he became very sad, because he was very rich. As the Lord Jesus looked upon him, He commented on the difficulty of those that have riches entering into the kingdom of God. The difficulty is in having riches without loving them and without trusting them.

This whole section raises disturbing questions for Christians as well as for unbelievers. How can we be said truly to love our neighbors when we live in wealth and comfort when others are perishing for want of the gospel of Christ?

Jesus said that it is easier for a camel to go through the eye of a needle than for a rich man to enter into the kingdom of God. Many explanations have been given of this statement. Some have suggested that the needle's eye is a small inner gate in the wall of a city, and that a camel could enter only by kneeling down. However, the meaning of the Lord's statement seems to lie on the surface. Just as it is impossible for a camel to go through the eye of a needle, so it is impossible for a rich man to enter into the kingdom of God. It is not enough to explain this as meaning that a rich man cannot, by his own efforts, enter the kingdom; that is true of rich and poor alike. The meaning seems to be that it is impossible for a man to enter the kingdom of God as a rich man; as long as he makes a god of his wealth, lets it stand between himself and his soul's salvation, he cannot be converted. The simple fact of the matter is that not many rich people are saved, and those who are must first be broken before God.

As the disciples thought about all of this, they began to wonder who could be saved. To them, riches had always been a sign of God's blessing (Deut. 28:1-8). If rich Jews aren't saved, then who can be? The Lord answered that God could do what man cannot do. In other words, God can take a greedy, grasping, ruthless materialist, remove his love for gold, and substitute for it a true love for the Lord. It is a miracle of divine grace.

The servant is not above his Master; the Lord Jesus abandoned His heavenly riches in order to save our guilty souls. It is not fitting for followers of Christ to be rich in a world where He was poor. The value of souls, the imminence of Christ's return, and love for Christ should lead us to invest every possible material asset in His work.

When Peter reminded the Lord that the disciples had left their homes and families to follow Him, the Lord replied that such a life of sacrifice is rewarded liberally in this life, and will be further rewarded in the eternal state. The latter part of verse 30 ("and in the age to come eternal life,") does not mean that eternal life is gained by forsaking all; rather, it refers to increased capacity for enjoying the glories of heaven, plus increased rewards in the heavenly kingdom. It means the full realization of the life that had been received at the time of conversion.

Jesus Predicts His Death and Resurrection (18:31-34)

For the third time, Jesus took the disciples aside and warned them in detail what awaited Him (see 9:22, 44). He predicted His passion as being in fulfillment of what the prophets of the Old Testament had written. With divine foresight, He calmly prophesied that He would be delivered up to the Gentiles. "It was more probable that He would be privately slain, or stoned to death in a tumult."[2] But the prophets had foretold His betrayal, His being mocked, shamefully treated and spit upon, and so it must be. He would be scourged and killed, but the third day He would rise again.

The remaining chapters unfold the drama that He so wonderfully foreknew and foretold: Their going to Jerusalem (18:35-19:46); The Son of Man would be delivered to the Gentiles (19:47-23:1); He would be shamefully treated (23:1-32); they would put Him to death (23:33-56); the third day He would rise again (24:1-12).

The disciples understood none of these things. The meaning of Jesus' words was hidden from them. They did not enter into the significance of what He said. It seems hard for us to understand why they were so dull in this matter, but the reason is probably this: Their minds were so filled with thoughts of a temporal deliverer who would rescue them from the control of Rome, and set up the kingdom immediately, that they refused to entertain any other program. We often believe what we want to believe, and resist the truth if it does not fit into our preconceived ideas.

> We often believe what we want to believe, and resist the truth if it does not fit into our preconceived ideas.

A Blind Beggar Receives Sight (18:35-43)

The Lord Jesus had now left Perea by crossing the Jordan and had come to the vicinity of Jericho. Luke says the incident that follows took place as He was approaching Jericho. Matthew and Mark say that it is when He was leaving the city (Matt. 20:29; Mark 10:46). Also Matthew says that there were two blind men; Mark and Luke both say there was one. It is possible that Luke is speaking of the new city, whereas Matthew and Mark are referring to the old city. It is also possible that there was more than one miracle of the blind receiving their sight. Whatever the true explanations might be, we confidently believe that if our knowledge were greater, the seeming contradictions would disappear.

Luke tells us that a blind beggar somehow recognized Jesus to be the Messiah because he addressed Him as the Son of David. He asked Jesus to have mercy on him, that is, to restore his sight. In spite of the attempts of some to silence the beggar, he insistently cried to the Lord Jesus. The people were not interested in a beggar, but Jesus was.

Commenting on the phrase in verse 40, "And Jesus stood still," Darby says, "Joshua once bade the sun stand still in the heavens, but here the *Lord* of the sun, and the moon, and the heavens, stands still at the bidding of a blind beggar."

At Jesus' command some men brought the beggar to Him. Jesus asked him what he wanted. Without hesitation and without engaging in generalizations, the beggar replied that he wanted his sight. His prayer was short, specific, and full of faith. The Lord Jesus then granted the request, and the man received his sight immediately. Not only so, he followed the Lord, glorifying God.

We may learn from this incident that we should dare to believe God for the impossible. Great faith greatly honors Him. As the poet has written:

> Thou art coming to a King,
> Great petitions with thee bring;
> For His love and power are such,
> None can ever ask too much.

---

[1] Roy Hession, *The Calvary Road* (Philadelphia: Christian Literature Crusade, n.d.) p. 49.
[2] John Charles Ryle, *op. cit.*, p. 282.

10

ON TO JERUSALEM
(19:1–20:47)

The Conversion of Zacchaeus (19:1-10)

The conversion of Zacchaeus illustrates the truth of verse 27 of the previous chapter, "The things which are impossible with men are possible with God." Zacchaeus was a rich man, and ordinarily it is impossible for a rich man to enter the kingdom of God. But Zacchaeus humbled himself before Christ and did not let his wealth come between his soul and God.

It was when Jesus was passing through Jericho on His third and final trip to Jerusalem that Zacchaeus tried to see Him. This was undoubtedly the seeking of curiosity (v. 3). Although he was a chief man among the tax-collectors, he was not embarrassed to do something unconventional in order to see Jesus. Because he was a short man, he knew he would be hindered from getting a good view of Jesus. So he ran on ahead, and climbed a mulberry (sycamore) tree alongside the route the Lord was taking. This act of faith did not go unnoticed. As Jesus came near, He looked into the tree and saw Zacchaeus there. He ordered him to come down quickly, and invited Himself to the tax-collector's house. This is the only case on record where Christ invited Himself to a home. Zacchaeus did as he was told, and received the Lord joyfully. We can almost certainly date his conversion from this time.

The Savior's critics were incensed by this incident. They murmured against Jesus because He went to stay in the home of a man who was known to be a sinner. They overlooked the fact that, coming into a world like ours, He was limited exclusively to homes like that. Salvation had brought a radical change in the life of Zacchaeus. He informed Jesus that he now intended to give half his goods to the poor. (Up to this time, he had been gouging as much as possible from the poor.) He also planned to make four-fold restitution for any money he had gained dishonestly. This was more than the law demanded (Ex. 22:4, 7; Lev. 6:5; Num. 5:7). It showed that Zacchaeus was now controlled by love, whereas formerly he was mastered by covetousness. There was no doubt that Zacchaeus had taken things dishonestly. Kenneth Wuest translates verse 8b: "And since I have wrongfully exacted . . ." No "if" about it (the word "if" often has the meaning of "since.").

In verse 8, it almost sounds as if Zacchaeus were boasting of his philanthropy and trusting in this for his salvation. That is not the point at all. He was saying that his new life in Christ made him desire to make restitution for the past, and that in gratitude to God for forgiving him, he now wanted to use his money for the glory of God and for the blessing of his neighbors. This verse is one of the strongest in the Bible on the subject of restitution. Salvation does not relieve a person from making right the wrongs of the past. Debts contracted during one's unconverted days are not cancelled by the new birth. And if money was stolen before salvation, then a true sense of the grace of God requires that this money be repaid after a person has become a child of God.

> *Salvation does not relieve a person from making right the wrongs of the past.*

In verse 9, Jesus plainly announced that salvation had come to the house of Zacchaeus, because he was a son of Abraham. We should be clear at this point to understand that salvation did not come because Zacchaeus was a Jew by birth. Here the expression "a son of Abraham" indicates more than natural descent; it means that Zacchaeus exercised the same kind of faith in the Lord that Abraham did. Also, it should be clearly understood that salvation did not come to Zacchaeus's home because of his charity and restitution, described in verse 8. These things are the effect of salvation, not the cause. Then in answer to those who criticized Jesus for lodging with a sinner, Jesus said, "The Son of Man has come to seek and to save that which was lost." In other words, the conversion of Zacchaeus was a fulfillment of the very purpose of Christ's coming into the world.

The Parable of the Ten Pounds (19:11-27)

As Jesus neared Jerusalem from Jericho, many of His followers thought the kingdom would be set up soon. In the parable of the ten minas (pounds), He dispelled such hopes. The parable showed that there would be an interval between His first and second advents during which His disciples were to be occupied for Him. The parable of the nobleman had an actual historical parallel in the history of Archelaus. He was chosen by Herod to be his successor but was rejected by the people. He went away to Rome to have his appointment confirmed, then returned, rewarded his servants and destroyed his enemies.

In the parable, Jesus Himself is the "certain nobleman" who went to heaven to await the time when He would return and set up His kingdom upon the earth. The ten servants typify His disciples. He gave each one a mina and told them to trade with this until He came again. While there are differences in the talents and abilities of the servants of the Lord (see the parable of the talents in Matthew 25:14-30), there are some things that they have in common, such as the privileges of sharing the gospel and representing Christ to the world. Doubtless the mina speaks of these.

The citizens represent the Jewish nation. They not only rejected Him, but even after His departure, they sent a message after Him saying, "We will not have this man to reign over us." This message might very well represent their treatment of Christ's servants such as Stephen and other martyrs. In verse 15, the Lord is seen, in type, returning to set up His kingdom. Then He will reckon with those to whom He gave the pounds.

Believers in this present age will be reviewed as far as their service is concerned at the judgment seat of Christ. This takes place in heaven, following the rapture. The faithful Jewish remnant who will witness for Christ during the tribulation period will be reviewed at Christ's second advent. This is the judgment that seems to be primarily in view in this passage.

The first servant had earned ten minas with the one mina that had been entrusted to him. He was aware that the money was not his own ("your mina") and he used it as best he could in the advancement of his master's interests. The master praised him as being faithful in a very little—a reminder that after we have done our best we are unprofitable servants. His reward was to have authority over ten cities. This seems to indicate that rewards for faithful service are linked with rule in Christ's kingdom.

The extent to which a disciple will rule is determined by the measure of his devotion and self-expenditure. The second servant had earned five minas with his original mina. His reward was to rule over five cities.

The third came with nothing but excuses. He returned the mina, carefully preserved. He had earned nothing with it. Why not? He as much as blamed the nobleman for it. He said he knew the nobleman was a harsh person who expected returns without expenditure. But his own words condemned him, even if they were not true. If he thought the nobleman was like that, the least he could have done was to turn the mina over to a bank that it might earn some interest. In quoting the words of the nobleman in verse 22, Jesus did not admit that they were true of Him. It was simply the sinful heart of the servant that blamed the master for his own laziness. But if he really believed them he should have acted accordingly. In verse 23, there seems to be the suggestion that we should either put everything we have to work for the Lord, or we should turn it over to someone else who will use it for Him.

The nobleman's verdict on the third servant was to take the mina from him and give it to the first who had earned the ten minas. If we don't use our opportunities for the Lord, they will be taken from us. On the other hand, if we are faithful in a very little, God will see that we will never lack the means to serve Him even more. It may seem unfair to some that the mina was given to the man who already had ten minas, but it is a fixed principle in the spiritual life that those who love Him and serve Him passionately are given ever-widening areas of opportunity. Failure to buy up the opportunities results in a loss of all.

The third servant suffered a loss of reward, but no other punishment is specified. There is no question as to his salvation. The citizens who would not have the nobleman as their ruler are denounced as enemies and doomed to death. This was a said prediction of the fate of the nation that had rejected the Messiah.

Jesus Approaches Jerusalem (19:28-40)

It was now the Sunday before His crucifixion. Jesus had drawn near to the eastern slope of the Mount of Olives on His way to Jerusalem. When He approached Bethphage and Bethany, He sent two of the disciples into a village to get a colt for His entrance into Jerusalem. He told them exactly where they would find the animal and what the owners would say. After the disciples had explained their mission, the owners seemed quite willing to release their colt for use by Jesus. Perhaps they had been blessed previously by the ministry of the Lord and had offered to be of help to Him anytime He needed it.

The disciples made a cushion or saddle for the Lord with their clothing, then spread garments on the way before Him as He ascended from the western base of the Mount of Olives to Jerusalem. Then with one accord the followers of Jesus burst out in praise for all the mighty works they had seen Him do. They hailed Him as God's King, and chanted that the effect of His coming was peace in heaven and glory in the highest. It is significant that they cried "Peace in heaven" rather than "Peace on earth." There could not be peace on earth, because the Prince of Peace had been rejected and was soon to be slain. But there would be peace in heaven as a result of the impending death of Christ on Calvary's cross and His ascension to heaven.

The Pharisees were angry that Jesus should be publicly honored in this way. They suggested that He should silence them. But Jesus answered that such acclamation was inevitable. If the disciples wouldn't do it, the stones would. He thus rebuked the Pharisees for being more hard and unresponsive than the inanimate stones.

Jesus Weeps Over the City (19:41-44)

As Jesus drew near to Jerusalem, He uttered a lamentation over the city that had missed its golden opportunity. If the people had only received Him as Messiah, it would have meant peace for them. But they didn't recognize that Jesus was the source of peace. Now it was too late. They had already determined what they would do with the Son of God. Because of their rejection of Him, their eyes were blinded. Because they *would* not see Him, they *could* no longer see Him.

> The Jews didn't recognize that Jesus was the source of peace.

Pause here to reflect on the wonder of the Savior's tears. As W. H. Griffith Thomas has said, "Let us sit at Christ's feet until we learn the wonder of His tears and beholding the sins and sorrows of city and countryside, weep over them too."

In verses 43 and 44, Jesus gave a solemn preview of the siege of Titus—how that Roman general would encircle the city, trap the inhabitants, massacre both young and old, and level the walls and buildings. Not one stone would be left on top of another. And it was all because Jerusalem "did not know the time of its visitation." Jesus had visited the city with the offer of salvation. But the people did not want Him. They had no room for Him in their scheme of things.

The Second Cleansing of the Temple (19:45-46)

Jesus had cleansed the temple at the outset of His public ministry as recorded in John 2:14-17. Now as His ministry rapidly drew to a close, He entered the sacred precincts and cast out those who were making the house of prayer into a den of thieves. The danger of introducing commercialism into the things of God is always present. Christendom today is riddled by this evil. Church bazaars and suppers, organized financial drives, preaching for profit—and all in the Name of Christ! Notice that Christ quoted Scripture to support His action (see Isaiah 56:7 and Jeremiah 7:11).

The Religious Leaders Are Frustrated (19:47-48)

Each day Jesus taught in the temple area—not inside the temple, but in the courts where the public was allowed. The Jewish leaders longed for some excuse to destroy Him, but the common people were still captivated by the miracle-working Nazarene. His time had not yet come. But soon the hour would strike, and then the chief priests, scribes, and Pharisees would close in for the kill.

It is now Monday. Tuesday, the last day of His public teaching, is described in 20:1-22:6.

Jesus Silences the Priests and Scribes (20:1-8)

What a picture: the Master Teacher tirelessly proclaiming the good news in the shadow of the temple, and the leaders of Israel insolently challenging His right to teach! To them, Jesus was a simple carpenter from Nazareth. He had no formal education, no academic degrees, no accreditation by an ecclesiastical body. What were His credentials? Who gave Him authority to teach and preach to others and to cleanse the temple? These were the things they wanted to know.

Jesus answered by asking them a question; if they had answered correctly, they would have answered their own question. Was John's ministry approved by God, or was it merely of human authority? They were caught. If they acknowledged that John preached with divine authority, then why didn't they obey the message by repenting and receiving the Messiah whom he proclaimed? But if they said John was just another professional preacher, they would stir up the anger of the crowd, who still acknowledged John to be a prophet of God. So they said, "We don't know where John got his authority." Jesus said, "Neither will I tell you by what authority I do these things." If they couldn't tell that much about John, why did they question the authority of One who was greater than John?

This passage shows that the great essential in teaching God's Word is to be filled with the Holy Spirit. If a man has that enabling, he can triumph over those whose power is wrapped up in degrees and human titles and honors. "Where did you get your diploma? Who ordained you?" The old question is still being asked. The successful gospel preacher who has not trodden the theological halls of some distinguished university or elsewhere is, even today, challenged on the points of his fitness and the validity of his ordination.

The Parable of the Vineyard (20:9-18)

The insistent yearning of the heart of God over the nation of Israel is told out once again in this parable of the vineyard. God is the man who let out the vineyard (Israel) to vinedressers (the leaders of the nation) (see Isaiah 5:1-7). He sent servants to these servants to get some fruit for Himself; these servants were the prophets of God, like Isaiah and John the Baptist, who had tried to call Israel to repentance and faith. But Israel's rulers invariably persecuted the prophets.

Finally, God sent His beloved Son, with the express thought that they would respect Him (although God knew, of course, that Christ would be rejected). Notice that Christ distinguishes Himself from all others. They were servants; He is the Son.

True to their past history, the vinedressers determined to get rid of the Son. They wanted exclusive rights as leaders and teachers of the people: "that the inheritance may be ours." They would not surrender their religious position to Jesus. If they killed Him, their power in Israel would be unchallenged—or so they thought. So they cast Him out of the vineyard and killed Him.

At this point in the story, Jesus asked His Jewish hearers what the owner of the vineyard would do to such wicked husbandmen. In Matthew's gospel, the chief priests and elders condemned themselves by answering that he would kill them (Matt. 21:41). Here the Lord Himself supplied the answer, "He will come and destroy those vinedressers and give the vineyard to others." This meant that the Christ-rejecting Jews would be destroyed, and that God would take others into their place of privilege. The "others" may refer to the Gentiles or to regenerated Israel of the last days. The Jews recoiled at such a suggestion. "Certainly not!" they said. Jesus confirmed the prediction by quoting Psalm 118:22. The Jewish builders had rejected Christ, the Stone. They had no place in their plans for Him. But God was determined that He would have the place of preeminence, by making Him the Head of the corner. Although it is difficult to state definitely what the head of the corner is in architecture, it is certain that it is a stone which is indispensable and in a place of greatest honor.

The two comings of Christ are indicated in verse 18. His first advent is depicted as a stone on the ground; men stumbled at His humiliation and lowliness, and they were broken to pieces for rejecting Him. In the second part of the verse, the stone is seen falling from heaven and scattering unbelievers as dust.

Christ's Enemies Are Outwitted Again (20:19-26)

The scribes and chief priests realized that Jesus had been speaking against them, so they became more intent to seize Him. They sent spies to trick Him into saying something for which He could be arrested and tried by the Roman governor. These spies first praised Him as one who would be faithful to God at any cost and fearless of man (hoping He would speak against Caesar). Then they asked Him if it was right for a Jew to pay taxes to Caesar. If Jesus said no, then they would accuse Him of treason and turn Him over to the Romans for trial. If He said yes, He would alienate the Herodians (and the great mass of the Jews for that matter). Jesus discerned the plot against Him. He asked them for a denarius; perhaps He did not own one Himself. At any rate, the fact that they possessed and used these coins showed their bondage to a Gentile power.

"Whose image and inscription does it have?" Jesus asked. They admitted it was Caesar's. Then Jesus silenced them with the command, "Render therefore to Caesar the things that are Caesar's, and to God the things that are God's." They were seemingly so concerned about Caesar's interests but they were not nearly so concerned about God's interests. "The money belongs to Caesar, and you belong to God. Let the world have its coins, but let God have His creatures."

——————— ✑ ———————
Let the world have its coins, but let God have His creatures.
——————— ✑ ———————

It is so easy to quibble over minor matters while neglecting the main things in life. And it is so easy to discharge our debts to our fellow-men while robbing God of His rightful dues.

The Sadducees Are Confounded (20:27-44)

Since the attempt to trap Jesus in a political question failed, the Sadducees next came to Him with a theological quibble. They denied the possibility of the bodies of the dead ever being raised again, so they tried by an extreme illustration to make the doctrine of resurrection appear ridiculous.

They reminded Jesus that in the law of Moses a single man was supposed to marry his brother's widow in order to carry on the family name and preserve the family property (Lev. 18:16; 20:21; Deut. 25:5). A woman married seven brothers in succession, according to their story. When the seventh died, she was still childless. Then she also died. In the resurrection, whose wife would she be? That is what they wanted to know.

They thought they were so clever in posing such an unanswerable problem. Jesus answered that the marriage relationship was for this life only; it would not be continued in heaven. He did not say that husbands and wives would not recognize each other in heaven, but their relationship there would be on a completely different basis. The expression "those who are counted worthy to attain that age" does not suggest that any people are personally worthy for heaven; the only worthiness sinners can have is the worthiness of the Lord Jesus Christ. "Those are counted worthy who judge themselves, who vindicate Christ, and who own that all worthiness belongs to Him."[1] The phrase "resurrection from the dead" refers to a resurrection of believers only. It really means resurrection *out from* the dead ones. The idea of a general resurrection in which all the dead, both saved and unsaved, are raised at one time, is not found in the Bible.

The superiority of the celestial state is further indicated in verse 36. There is no more death; in that respect, men will be like the angels. Also, they will be manifested as sons of God. Believers are sons of God already, but not to outward observance. In heaven, they will be visibly manifested as sons of God. The fact that they participated in the first resurrection insures this. "We know that, when He is revealed, we shall be like Him, for we shall see Him as He is" (1 John 3:2). "When Christ who is our life appears, then you also will appear with Him in glory" (Colossians 3:4).

To prove the resurrection Jesus referred to Exodus 3:6 where Moses quoted Jehovah as calling Himself the God of Abraham, Isaac and Jacob. Now if the Sadducees would just stop to think, they would realize that God is the God of the living, not of the dead, and that Abraham, Isaac and Jacob were all dead. The necessary conclusion is that God must raise them from the dead. The Lord did not say, "I *was* the God of Abraham . . . ," but "I *am* . . ." The character of God as the God of the living demands the resurrection.

Some of the scribes had to admit the force of the argument (vv. 39-40). But Jesus was not finished; once again He appealed to God's Word. In Psalm 110:1, David called the Messiah his Lord. The Jews generally agreed that the Messiah would be David's son. How could He be David's Lord and David's son at the same time? The Lord Jesus Himself was the answer to the question. He was descended from David as Son of Man; yet He was David's Creator. But they were too blind to see.

Jesus Warns Against the Scribes (20:45-47)

Jesus then publicly warned the crowd against the scribes. They wore long robes, giving the impression they were pious. They loved to be called by distinguished titles as they walked through the market places. They maneuvered to get places of prominence in the synagogues and at banquets. But they robbed defenseless widows of their life savings, covering up their wickedness by long prayers. Such hypocrisy would be punished all the more severely.

---

[1] C. A. Coates, *op. cit.*, p. 252.

11

THE PLOT THICKENS
(21:1–22:71)

The Widow's Mite (21:1-4)

As Jesus watched the people depositing their gifts in the treasury of the temple, He was struck by the contrast between the rich men and a certain poor widow. They gave some, but she gave all. In God's estimation, she gave more than all of them put together. They gave out of their abundance; she gave out of her deep poverty. They gave what cost them little or nothing; she gave all the living that she had. Dr. Joseph Parker has said, "The gold of affluence which is given because it is not needed, God hurls to the bottomless pit; but the copper tinged with blood He lifts and kisses into the gold of eternity."

> In God's estimation, the widow gave more than all of the rich men put together.

Outline of Future Events (21:5-11)

From verse 5 through verse 33 we have a great prophetic discourse. Although it resembles the Olivet Discourse in Matthew 24 and 25, it is not identical. In this discourse, we find Jesus speaking alternately of the destruction of Jerusalem in AD 70 and then of the conditions that will precede His second advent. It is an illustration of the law of double reference—His predictions had an immediate and partial fulfillment in the siege of Titus, but they will have a further and complete fulfillment at the end of the tribulation period.

The outline of the discourse seems to be as follows:

1. Jesus foretells the destruction of Jerusalem (vv. 5-6).

2. The disciples ask when this will happen (v. 7).

3. Jesus first gives a general picture of events preceding His own second advent (vv. 8-11).

4. He then gives a picture of the fall of Jerusalem and the age that would follow (vv. 12-24).

5. Finally, He tells the signs that would precede His second coming and urges His followers to live in the expectation of His return (vv. 25-26).

As some of the people were admiring the magnificence of Herod's temple, Jesus warned them not to be preoccupied with material things that would soon pass away. The days were coming when the temple would be completely leveled. The disciples immediately wanted to know when this would happen and what sign would indicate it was about to happen. Their question undoubtedly referred exclusively to the destruction of Jerusalem.

Christ's answer first seemed to take them ahead to the end of the age when the temple would again be destroyed prior to the setting up of the kingdom. There would be false messiahs and false rumors, wars, and uprisings. "But the end will not come immediately" means it is not immediate. There would not only be conflict among nations, but great catastrophes of nature, like earthquakes, famines, plagues, terrors, and great signs from heaven.

The Period Before the End (21:12-19)

In the preceding section, Jesus had described events immediately preceding the end of the age. Verse 12 is introduced by the expression "But before all these things . . ." So verses 12-24 describe the period between the time of the discourse and the future tribulation period.

His disciples would be arrested, persecuted, tried before religious and civil powers, and imprisoned. It might seem like failure and tragedy to them, but actually the Lord would overrule it to make it a testimony for His glory. They were not to prepare their defense in advance. In the crisis hour, God would give them special wisdom to say things that would completely confound their accusers. There would be treachery within families; unsaved relatives would betray Christians, and some would even be killed because of their stand for Christ.

There is a seeming contradiction between verse 16, "They will put some of you to death," and verse 18, "But not a hair of your head shall be lost." It can only mean that though some would die as martyrs for Christ, their spiritual preservation would be complete. They would die but they would not perish.

> ──────── ❧ ────────
> **Those who are genuinely saved will stand true and loyal at any cost.**
> ──────── ❧ ────────

Verse 19 should read, "In your patience you shall keep your souls." It does not mean to keep one's soul in a state of patience. Rather, it indicates that those who patiently endure for Christ rather than renouncing Him will thus prove the reality of their faith. Those who are genuinely saved will stand true and loyal at any cost.

The Doom of Jerusalem (21:20-24)

Now Jesus clearly takes up the subject of the destruction of Jerusalem in AD 70. This event would be signaled by the city's being surrounded by the Roman armies.

"The Christian of an early day—the year AD 70—had a specific sign to introduce the destruction of Jerusalem and the razing of the beautiful marble temple: 'When ye shall see Jerusalem compassed with armies, then know that the desolation thereof is nigh.' This was to be a positive sign of the destruction of Jerusalem, and at that sign they were to flee. Unbelief might have argued that with a besieging army outside the walls, escape would be impossible; but God's Word never fails. The Roman general withdrew his armies for a short season, thus giving the believing Jews the opportunity to escape. This they did, and went out to a place called Pella, where they were preserved."[1]

Any attempt to re-enter the city would be fatal. The city was about to be punished for its rejection of the Son of God. Pregnant women and nursing mothers would be at a distinct disadvantage; they would be hindered in escaping from the judgment of God upon the land of Israel and upon the Jewish people. Many would be killed, and the survivors would be carried off as captives in other lands.

The latter part of verse 24 is a remarkable prophecy that the ancient city of Jerusalem would be subject to Gentile rule from that time until Christ's return. It does not mean that the Jews might not control it for brief periods; the thought is that it would be continually subject to Gentile invasion and interference until the times of the Gentiles are fulfilled.

The New Testament distinguishes between the riches of the Gentiles, the fullness of the Gentiles, and the times of the Gentiles. The *riches* of the Gentiles (Rom. 11:12) refers to the place of privilege that the Gentiles enjoy at the present time while Israel is temporarily set aside by God. The *fullness* of the Gentiles (Rom. 11:25) is the time of the rapture, when Christ's Gentile bride will be completed and taken from the earth and when God will resume His dealings with Israel. The *times* of the Gentiles (Luke 21:24) really began with the Babylon captivity, 586 BC, and will extend to the time when Gentile nations will no longer assert control over the city of Jerusalem, namely, when Christ returns as King of kings and Lord of lords.

> Down through the centuries, Jerusalem has been largely controlled by Gentile powers.

Down through the centuries, from the time of Christ's words, Jerusalem has been largely controlled by Gentile powers. Julian, the Apostate (AD 331-363), sought to discredit Christianity by disproving this prophecy of the Lord. He therefore encouraged the Jews to rebuild the temple. They went to the work eagerly, using even silver shovels in their extravagance, and carrying the dirt in purple veils. But when they were working they were interrupted by an earthquake and by balls of fire coming from the ground. They had to abandon the project.[2]

Some Signs of Christ's Coming (21:25-28)

These verses describe the convulsions of nature and the cataclysms on earth that will precede Christ's second coming. There will be disturbances involving the sun, moon, and stars that will be clearly visible on earth. Heavenly bodies will be moved out of their orbits. They might cause the earth to be tilted off its axis. There will be great tidal waves sweeping over land areas. Panic will seize mankind because of heavenly bodies on a near-collision course with the earth. This is all suggested in verse 25. Then Christ will appear in a cloud with power and great glory. Believers will know His coming is near when the events described above begin to take place.

The Fig Tree and All the Trees (21:29-33)

Another sign indicating the nearness of His return is the shooting forth of the fig tree and all the trees. The fig tree is an apt picture of the nation of Israel; it would begin to evidence new life in the last days. Surely it is not without significance that after centuries of dispersal and obscurity, the nation of Israel was re-established in 1948, and is now recognized as a member of the family of nations. The shooting forth of the other trees may symbolize the phenomenal growth of nationalism and the emergence of many new governments in newly developed countries of the world. These signs would mean that Christ's glorious kingdom would soon be set up.

In verse 32, Jesus said that this generation would not pass away till all things be accomplished. But what did He mean by "this generation"? Some feel He referred to the generation living at the time He spoke these words, and that all things were fulfilled at the destruction of Jerusalem. But this cannot be so because there were no signs in the heavens at that time, and Christ did not return in a cloud with power and great glory.

Others suggest that "this generation" refers to the people living when these signs begin to take place, and that those who live to see the beginning of the signs would live to see the return of Christ. All the events predicted would happen within one generation. This is a possible explanation. Most likely, "this generation" refers to the Jewish people in their attitude of hostility to Christ. The Lord was saying that the Jewish race would survive, scattered yet indestructible, and that its attitude toward Him would not change down through the centuries. The atmospheric and stellar heavens would pass away—so would the earth in its present form—but these predictions of the Lord Jesus would not go unfulfilled (v. 33).

A Warning to Watch and Pray (21:34-38)

In the meantime, His disciples should guard against becoming so occupied with eating, drinking and mundane affairs that His coming might come unexpectedly. That is the way it will come on all those who think of the earth as their permanent dwelling place.

True disciples should watch and pray at all times, thus separating themselves from the ungodly world which is doomed to experience the wrath of God, and identifying themselves with those who shall stand in acceptance before the Son of Man.

Each day, Jesus taught in the temple area. At night He slept on the Mount of Olives. He was homeless in the world He had made. In the morning, the people crowded around Him afresh to hear Him.

Continued Plotting Against Jesus (22:1-2)

The Feast of Unleavened Bread here refers to the period beginning with the Passover and extending for seven more days, during which no leavened bread was eaten. The Passover was held on the 14th of the month Nisan, the 1st month of the Jewish year. The seven days from the 15th of the month to the 21st were known as the Feast of Unleavened Bread, but here in verse 1 that name takes in the entire feast. If Luke had been writing primarily to Jews, it would not have been necessary for him to mention the connection between the Feast of Unleavened Bread and the Passover.

The chief priests and scribes were continuously plotting how they might put the Lord Jesus to death, but they realized that they must do it without causing a riot. They feared the people and knew that many of the people still held Jesus in high esteem.

The Betrayer's Bargain (22:3-6)

In verse 3, Satan is said to have entered into Judas Iscariot, one of the twelve disciples. In John 13:27, this action is said to have taken place after Jesus had handed him the piece of bread during the Passover meal. We conclude either that this took place in successive stages, or that Luke is emphasizing the fact rather than the exact time when it took place.

At any rate, Judas made a bargain with the chief priests and the captains, that is, the commanders of the Jewish guard of the temple. He had carefully worked out a plan by which he could deliver Jesus into their hands without causing a riot. The plan was entirely acceptable, and they agreed to give him money—thirty pieces of silver, as we learn elsewhere. So Judas left to work out the details of his treacherous scheme.

Preparation for the Passover (22:7-13)

There are definite problems in connection with the various time periods mentioned in these verses. The day of unleavened bread would normally be thought of as the 13th of Nisan when all leavened bread had to be put away from a Jewish home. But here it says it was the day on which the Passover must be sacrificed, and that would make it the 14th of Nisan. No completely satisfactory explanation is available. Probably the events of the final Thursday begin here and continue through verse 53.

The Lord sent Peter and John into the city of Jerusalem to make preparations for the celebration of the Passover meal. He showed His complete knowledge of all things in His instructions to them. Once inside the city, they would meet a man bearing a pitcher of water. This was an unusual sight in an eastern city; it was usually the women who carried the pitchers of water. Doubtless the man here is a picture of the Holy Spirit, who leads seeking souls to the place of communion with the Lord.

Jesus not only foreknew the location and route of this man, but He also knew that a certain homeowner would be willing to make his large upper room available to Him and to the disciples. This man must have known Jesus and must have made a total commitment of his person and possessions to Him.

Everything was as He had predicted, and the disciples made all the necessary preparations.

There is a difference between the guest chamber (v. 11) and the large upper room (v. 12). The generous host provided better facilities than the disciples expected. When Jesus was born in Bethlehem, there was no guest chamber for Him in the inn (Greek *Kataluma*). Here He told His disciples to ask for a guest chamber (same Greek word), but they were given something better—a large and furnished upper room.

The Passover (22:14-18)

> _____ ❧ _____
>
> **The Lord Jesus Christ was the true Passover Lamb.**
>
> _____ ❧ _____

For centuries, the Jews had celebrated the Passover feast, commemorating their glorious deliverance from Egypt and from death through the blood of the spotless lamb. How vividly this must all have come before the mind of the Lord as He sat down with His disciples to keep the feast for the last time. He was the true Passover Lamb whose blood would soon be shed for the salvation of all who would trust in Him. "This Passover" (v. 15), that is, this particular one held inexpressible meaning for Him, and He had earnestly desired it before He suffered. He would not keep the Passover again until He returned to the earth and set up His glorious kingdom.

"'With fervent desire I have desired' (v. 15). The Greek word carries the sense of ardent, passionate longing. Knox fittingly translates it, 'I have longed and longed.' In these revealing words, Jesus invites all His disciples of every time and place to consider how passionately His heart longs for communion with us at His table."[3]

When someone handed a cup of wine to Him as part of the Passover ritual, He gave thanks for it and passed it to the disciples, reminding them once again that He would not drink of the fruit of the vine again until His millennial reign. The description of the Passover meal ends with verse 18.

The Lord's Supper (22:19-23)

The bread was a symbol of His body that would shortly be given for them.

The last Passover was immediately followed by the Lord's Supper. The Lord Jesus instituted this sacred memorial so that His followers down through the centuries would thus remember Him in His death. He first of all gave them the bread, a symbol of His body that would shortly be given for them. Then the cup spoke eloquently of His precious blood, which would be shed on the cross of Calvary. He spoke of it as the cup of the New Testament in His blood that was poured out for His own. This means that the new covenant, which He made primarily with the nation of Israel, was ratified by His blood. The complete fulfillment of the new covenant will take place during the kingdom of our Lord Jesus Christ on earth, but we as believers enter into the good of it at the present time.

The wine was representative of His precious blood.

The bread and wine were typical or representative of His body and blood. His body had not yet been given, neither had His blood been shed. Therefore it is incorrect to suggest that the symbols were miraculously changed into the realities. The Jewish people were forbidden to eat blood, and the disciples knew therefore that He was not speaking of literal blood, but of what pictured His blood.

It seems clear from verse 21 that Judas was actually present at the last supper. However, in John 13, it appears equally clear that the betrayer left the room after Jesus had handed the bread to him. The bread was dipped in the gravy of the Passover meal. Since this took place before the institution of the Lord's Supper, many believe that Judas was not actually present when the bread and wine were passed.

The sufferings and death of the Lord Jesus were inevitable, but it was not inevitable that Judas should be the one to betray Him. In this matter, Iscariot acted with the full consent of his will. That is why the Lord Jesus said, "Woe to that man by whom He [the Son of Man] is betrayed." Though Judas was one of the Twelve, he was not a true believer. Verse 23 reveals something of the surprise and self-distrust of the disciples. They did not know which of them would be guilty of this malicious act.

The Contest for Greatness (22:24-30)

It is a terrible indictment of the human heart that immediately following the Lord's Supper, the disciples should argue among themselves as to which of them was the greatest. The Lord Jesus reminded them that in His economy, greatness was the very opposite of man's idea. The kings who ruled over the Gentiles were commonly thought of as great persons; in fact they were called "Friends of the People." But it was only a title; actually, they were cruel tyrants. They had the name of greatness, but no personal characteristics to match it.

It was not to be so of the followers of the Lord. Those who would be great should take the place of the younger. And those who were chief should stoop in lowly service to others. These revolutionary dictums completely reversed the accepted traditions of the younger being inferior to the elder, and the chief manifesting greatness by mastery. In men's estimation, it was greater to be a guest at a meal than to serve the meal. But the Lord Jesus came as a servant of men, and all who would follow Him must imitate Him in this.

It was gracious of the Lord to commend the disciples for having continued with Him in His trials. They had just been quarreling among themselves. Very soon they would all forsake Him and flee. And yet He knew that in their hearts, they loved Him and that they had endured reproach for His Name's sake. Their reward would be to sit on thrones judging the twelve tribes of Israel when Christ returns to take the throne of David and rule over the earth. Just as surely as the Father had promised this kingdom to Christ, so surely would they reign with Him over the renewed earth.

Peter's Denial Foretold (22:31-34)

This is the last in a series of three dark chapters in the history of human faithlessness. The first was the treachery of Judas. The second was the selfish ambition of the disciples. Now we have the cowardice of Peter.

The repetition of Simon's name ("Simon, Simon") speaks of the love and tenderness of the heart of Christ for His vacillating disciple. Satan had asked to have all the disciples ("you," plural) that he might sift them as wheat. Jesus addressed Simon as representative of all. But the Lord Jesus had prayed for Simon ("you," singular) that his faith might not suffer an eclipse. Those are tremendous words, "I have prayed for you." After he "returned" to Christ, he was to strengthen his brethren. This "returning" relates to restoration. With unbecoming self-confidence, Peter expressed readiness to accompany Jesus to prison and to death. But he had to be told that before the morning light had fully dawned, he would deny three times that he even knew the Lord.

In Mark 14:30, the Lord is quoted as saying that before the cock crowed twice, Peter would deny Him three times. In Matthew 26:34, Luke 22:34, and John 13:38, the Lord said that before the cock crowed, Peter would deny Him three times. It is admittedly difficult to reconcile this seeming contradiction. It is possible that there was more than one cock-crowing, one during the night and another at dawn. Also it should be remembered that the gospels record at least six different denials by Peter. He denied Christ before a young woman (Matt. 26:69-70; Mark 14:66-68), before another young woman (Matt. 26:71-72; Mark 14:69-70), before the crowd that stood by (Matt. 26:73-74; Mark 14:70-71), before a man (Luke 22:58), before another man (Luke 22:59-60) and before a servant of the high priest (John 18:26-27). We know this man is different from the others because of what he said, that is, "Did I not see you in the garden with Him?"

New Marching Orders (22:35–38)

Earlier in His ministry, the Lord had instructed the disciples to go forth without purse, without food box, without comfortable shoes—the minimum. Bare essentials would be enough for them. And so it had proved. They had to confess that they had not lacked anything.

But now He was about to leave them, and they were to enter into a new phase of service for Him. They would be exposed to poverty, hunger, and danger, and it would be necessary for them to make provision for their current needs. They should now take a purse with money, a wallet or lunch box, and in the absence of a sword, they should sell their coats and buy one.

What did Jesus mean when He told the disciples to buy a sword? It seems clear that He could not have intended them to use the sword as an offensive weapon against other people. This would be in violation of His teaching in such passages as: "My kingdom is not of this world. If My kingdom were of this world, My servants would fight" (John 18:36). "All who take the sword will perish by the sword" (Matt. 26:52). "Love your enemies . . ." (Matt. 5:44) "Whoever slaps you on your right cheek, turn the other to him also" (Matt. 5:39). See also 2 Corinthians 10:4.

> What did Jesus mean when He told the disciples to buy a sword?

What then did Jesus mean by the sword? Some suggest that He was referring to the sword of the Spirit that is the word of God (Eph. 6:17). This is possible, but then the purse, the knapsack, and the garment should be spiritualized also. Williams says that the sword means the protection of an ordered government, pointing out that in Romans 13:4 it refers to the power of the magistrate. Lange says the sword is for defense against human enemies, but not for offense. But Matthew 5:39 seems to rule out the use of the sword, even for defensive purposes. Some think that the sword was for defense against wild animals only. This is possible. Verse 37 explains why it was necessary for the disciples to take these material things. The Lord had been with them up to this point, providing for their temporal needs. Soon He would be departing from them in accordance with the prophecy of Isaiah 53:12. The things concerning Him had an end, that is, His earthly life and ministry would come to a close by His being numbered with the transgressors.

The disciples completely misunderstood the Lord. They brought out two swords, implying that these would surely be enough for any problems that lay ahead. The Lord Jesus ended the conversation by saying "It is enough." They apparently thought that they could stop the attempt of His enemies to slay Him by using the swords. This was the farthest thought from His mind.

Jesus Prays in the Garden (22:39-46)

The Garden of Gethsemane was situated on the western slope of the Mount of Olives. Jesus often went there to pray, and the disciples (including the betrayer, of course) knew this.

At the conclusion of the Lord's Supper, Jesus and the disciples left the upper room and went to the garden. Once they were there, He warned them to pray that they should not enter into temptation. Perhaps the particular temptation He had in mind was the pressure to abandon God and His Christ when the enemies closed in.

Then Jesus left the disciples and went further into the garden where He prayed alone. His prayer was that if the Father were willing, this cup might pass from Him; nevertheless He wanted the will of God to be done, not His own. We understand this prayer to mean; if there is any other way by which sinners can be saved than by My going to the cross, reveal that way now. Of course, the heavens were silent, because there was no other way.

Christ's sufferings in the garden were not part of His atoning work. The work of redemption was accomplished during the three hours of darkness on the cross. But Gethsemane was in anticipation of Calvary. There the very thought of contact with our sins caused the Lord Jesus the keenest suffering. His perfect humanity is seen in the weakness which accompanied His distress. We read that an angel appeared to Him from heaven, strengthening Him. Only Luke records this fact, as well as the fact that His sweat became as great drops of blood. This latter detail caught the eye and interest of Luke, the careful physician. (It should be mentioned that verses 43 and 44 are omitted in some ancient manuscripts.) When the Lord Jesus returned to the disciples, they were sleeping. It was not the sleep of indifference, but rather the sleep of sorrowful exhaustion. Once again He urged them to rise and pray, because the crisis hour was drawing near, and they would be tempted to deny Him before the authorities.

> The very thought of contact with our sins caused the Lord Jesus the keenest suffering.

Judas Betrays Jesus (22:47-53)

By now, Judas had arrived with a group of the chief priests, elders, and captains of the temple to arrest the Lord. By prearrangement, the traitor was to mark out Jesus by kissing Him. "It was the crowning touch of horror, the last point of infamy beyond which human infamy could not go, when out in the garden Judas betrayed his Master, not with a shout or a blow or a stab, but with a kiss."[4] With infinite pathos Jesus asked Judas, "Are you betraying the Son of Man with a kiss?"

The disciples realized what was about to happen, and were ready to take the offensive. In fact one of them, Peter to be specific, took a sword and cut off the right ear of the servant of the high priest. Jesus rebuked him for using carnal means to fight a spiritual war. His hour had come, and God's predetermined purpose must be brought to pass. Tenderly and lovingly, Jesus touched the ear of the victim and healed him.

Turning to the Jewish leaders and officers, Jesus asked them why they came out after Him as if He were a fugitive criminal. Had He not taught daily in the temple area, yet they had not tried to take Him then? But He knew the answer. This was their hour, and the power of darkness.

It was now about midnight on Thursday.

> Jesus rebuked Peter for using carnal means to fight a spiritual war.

Peter Denies His Lord (22:54-62)

It seems that the religious trial of our Lord had three stages. First, He appeared before Annas. Then He appeared before Caiaphas. Finally He was arraigned before the Sanhedrin. The events from this point through verse 65 probably took place between 1 a.m. and 5 a.m. on Friday.

When the Lord was brought to the high priest's house, Peter followed at a distance. Inside, he took his place with those who were warming themselves at a fire in the center of the courtyard. A young woman looked across at Peter and exclaimed that he was one of the followers of Jesus. Pathetically Peter denied that he knew Him. Shortly afterwards, someone else pointed the accusing finger at Peter as one of the followers of Jesus of Nazareth. Again Peter denied the charge. About an hour later, someone else recognized Peter as a Galilean, and also as a disciple of the Lord. Peter denied any knowledge of what the man was talking about. But this time his denial was punctuated by the crowing of the rooster. In that dark moment, Peter's gaze met that of the Lord Jesus, and the disciple remembered the prediction that before the cock crew, he would deny Him thrice. The look from the Son of God sent Peter out into the night to weep bitterly.

Jesus Mishandled by Soldiers (22:63-65)

It was the officers assigned to the sacred temple in Jerusalem who had apprehended Jesus. Now these supposed guardians of God's holy house began to mock Jesus and to beat Him. After blindfolding Him, they struck Him, then asked Him to identify the one who did it. This is not all they did, but He patiently endured this contradiction of sinners against Himself.

Jesus Before the Council (22:66-71)

At daybreak (5-6 a.m.), the leaders led Jesus away to the council, or Sanhedrin. The members of the Sanhedrin asked Him outright if He were the Messiah. Jesus said, in effect, that it was useless to discuss the matter with them. They were not open to receive the truth. But He warned them that the One who stood before them in humiliation would one day be seated at the right hand of the power of God (see Psalm 110:1). Then they asked Him plainly if He were the Son of God. There is no question what they meant. To them, the Son of God was one who was equal with God. The Lord Jesus answered, "You rightly say that I am." In some versions it almost sounds as if He dodged the question. But what He actually said was, "You say that I am, and you are absolutely correct" (see Mark 14:62). That was all they needed. Had they not heard Him speak blasphemy, claiming equality with God? There was no further need for witnesses.

But there was a problem. In their law, the penalty for blasphemy was death. But the Jews were under Roman power and they did not have authority to put prisoners to death. So they had to take Jesus to Pilate, and he would not be the least bit interested in a religious charge such as blasphemy. So they had to prefer political charges against Him.

1   *Christian Truth Magazine*, November, 1962, p. 303.
2   Edward Gibbon, *The Decline and Fall of the Roman Empire*, Vol. II (Chicago: Belford, Charlese and Co., n.d.) pp. 95-101.
3   Daily Notes of the Scripture Union, October, 1965.
4   James S. Stewart, *op. cit.*, p. 154.

12

DEATH! RESURRECTION! GLORY!
(23:1–24:53)

The Trial Before Pilate (23:1-7)

Following His appearance before the Sanhedrin ("the whole multitude of them"), the Lord Jesus was hurried away to be put on civil trial before Pilate, the Roman governor. Three political charges were now brought against Him by the religious leaders. First of all, they accused Him of perverting the nation, that is, of turning the loyalty of the people away from Rome. Second, they said that he forbade Jews to pay tribute to Caesar. Finally, they accused Him of making Himself a king.

When Pilate asked Jesus if He was the King of the Jews, the Lord said that He was. Pilate did not interpret His claim as any threat to the Roman emperor. After a private interview with Jesus (John 18:33-38a), he turned to the chief priests and to the crowd saying that he could find no fault with Him. The mob became more insistent, accusing Jesus of stirring up disloyalty, beginning in despised Galilee even to Jerusalem. When Pilate heard the word Galilee, he thought he had found an escape route for himself. Galilee was Herod's jurisdiction, and so Pilate tried to avoid any further involvement in this case by turning Jesus over to Herod. It so happened that Herod was visiting in Jerusalem at that very time.

Questioned and Mocked by Herod (23:8-12)

Herod Antipas was the son of Herod the Great, who massacred the infants of Bethlehem. It was Antipas who murdered John the Baptist for condemning his illicit relationship with his brother's wife. This was the

Herod Jesus called "that fox" in Luke 13:32. Herod was quite happy to have Jesus appear before him. He had heard a great deal about Him, and for a long time he had wanted to see a miracle performed by Him.

No matter how much Herod questioned the Lord, he received no answer. The Jews became more violent in their accusations, but Jesus did not open His mouth. All Herod could do, he thought, was to allow his soldiers to manhandle Jesus, and to mock Him by clothing Him in a gorgeous robe and sending Him back to Pilate.

Up to this point, Herod and Pilate had been at enmity between themselves, but now the enmity was changed to friendship. They were both on the same side against the Lord Jesus, and this united them. "It is a matter of shame to Christians that while the devil can persuade wicked men to lay aside their enmities in order to do harm, Christians cannot even keep up friendship in order to do good" (Theophylact).

Pilate's Verdict: Innocent But Condemned (23:13-25)

Because he had failed to act righteously in acquitting his royal prisoner, Pilate now found himself deeply entrapped. He called a hurried meeting of the Jewish leaders and explained to them that neither Herod nor he had been able to find any evidence of disloyalty on the part of Jesus. "Nothing deserving of death has been done by Him," that is, by Jesus (v. 15). So he proposed to whip Jesus and then to let Him go. "This sorry compromise was, of course, totally unjustifiable and illogical. It was the poor, fear-driven soul's attempt to do his duty by Jesus and to please the crowd at the same time. But it did neither, and it is no wonder that the angry priests would not accept that verdict at any price."[1]

The chief priests and rulers were enraged. They demanded the death of Jesus and the release of Barabbas, a notorious criminal who had been imprisoned because of insurrection and murder. Again Pilate feebly attempted to exonerate the Lord but the vicious demands of the mob drowned him out. No matter what he said, they persisted in demanding the death of the Son of God. And although Pilate had already pronounced Jesus innocent, he now condemned Him to death in order to please the people. At the same time Barabbas was released to the multitude. (Verse 17 is omitted by some versions.)

Jesus Led to Calvary (23:26-32)

It was now approximately 9 a.m. on Friday.

On the way to the scene of crucifixion, the soldiers commanded a man named Simon of Cyrene to carry the cross. Not much is known of this man, but it appears that his two sons, Alexander and Rufus, afterwards became well-known Christians (Mark 15:21).

A crowd of sympathetic followers wept for Jesus as He was led away. Addressing the women in the crowd as daughters of Jerusalem, He told them that they should not pity Him but should pity themselves. He was referring, of course, to the terrible destruction that would descend on the city of Jerusalem in AD 70. The suffering and sorrow of those days would be so great that barren women, up till now an object of reproach, would be considered especially fortunate. The horrors of the siege of Titus would be such that people would wish for the mountains to fall on them, and for the hills to cover them.

Then the Lord Jesus added the words, "For if they do these things in the green wood, what will be done in the dry?" He Himself was the green tree, and unbelieving Israel was the dry. If the Romans heaped such shame and suffering upon the sinless, innocent Son of God, what dreadful punishment would fall upon the guilty murderers of God's beloved Son?

In the procession with Jesus were two criminals, also scheduled for execution.

The Crucifixion (23:33-38)

The place of execution was also called "The Skull." Perhaps the configuration of the land resembled a skull, or perhaps it was so named because it was the place of death, and a skull is often used as a symbol of death.

> The restraint of Scripture in describing the crucifixion is noteworthy.

The restraint of Scripture in describing the crucifixion is noteworthy. There is no lingering over the terrible details. There is just the simple statement, there they crucified Him. "That the Messiah should die was hard enough to believe, but that He should die such a death was utterly beyond belief. Yet so it was. Everything which Christ ever touched—the cross included—He adorned and transfigured and haloed with splendor and beauty; but let us never forget out of what appalling depths He had set the cross on high."[2]

There were three crosses at Calvary that day, the cross of Jesus in the middle, and a criminal's cross on each side of Him. Thus was fulfilled the Scripture, "He was numbered with the transgressors."

With infinite love and mercy, Jesus cried from the cross, "Father, forgive [meaning, "allow"] them, for they do not know what they do." Who knows what an avalanche of divine wrath was averted by this prayer! "In the soul of Jesus there was no resentment; no anger, no lurking desire for punishment upon the men who were maltreating Him. Men have spoken in admiration of the mailed fist. When I hear Jesus thus pray, I know that the only place for the mailed fist [i.e. threat of armed force] is in hell."[3]

After this, the soldiers divided His garments among them, and cast lots for His seamless robe.

The rulers stood before the cross, mocking Him, and challenging Him to save Himself if He really was the Messiah of God.

The soldiers too mocked Him, offering Him sour wine and challenging His ability to save Himself. Also they put a title at the head of the cross, "This is the King of the Jews." "We cannot miss the significance of the fact that the inscription was written in three languages, Greek and Latin, and Hebrew. No doubt that was done in order to make sure that everyone in the crowd might read it; but Christ's church has always seen in it, and rightly, a symbol of the universal lordship of her Master. For these were the great world languages, each of them the servant of one dominant idea. Greek was the language of culture and knowledge; in that realm, said the inscription, Jesus was King! Latin was the language of law and government; Jesus was King there! Hence even as He hung dying, it was true that 'on His head were many crowns' (Rev. 19:12)."[4]

The Two Thieves (23:39-43)

We learn from the other gospel narratives that both thieves reviled Jesus at the outset. If He was the Messiah, why did He not save them all? But then one of the thieves had a change of heart. Turning to his companion, he rebuked him for his irreverence. After all they were both suffering for crimes that they had committed. Their punishment was deserved. But this man on the middle cross had done nothing wrong. Turning to the Lord

Jesus, the thief asked to be remembered when Christ came back and set up His kingdom upon the earth. Such faith was remarkable. The dying thief believed that Jesus would rise from the dead and would eventually reign over the world. Jesus rewarded his faith with the promise that that very day, they would be together in Paradise. Paradise is the same as the third heaven (2 Cor. 12:2, 4), and means the dwelling place of God. "Today—what speed! With me—what company! In paradise—what felicity [happiness]!" (Williams).

"This story reveals the truth to us that salvation is conditioned upon repentance and faith. However, it contains other important messages also. It declares that salvation is independent of sacraments. The thief had never been baptized, nor had he partaken of the Lord's Supper. It is obvious that had he lived he would have carried out the requirements of his Lord by accepting these sacraments. He did in fact boldly profess his faith in the presence of a hostile crowd and amid the taunts and jeers of rulers and soldiers, yet he was saved without any formal rites. It is further evident that salvation is independent of good works. . . . It is also seen that there is no 'sleep of the soul.' The body may sleep, but consciousness exists after death. Out of a life of sin and shame, the penitent robber passed immediately into a state of blessedness. Again it may be remarked that salvation is not universal. There were two robbers; only one was saved. Last of all it may be noted that the very essence of the joy, which lies beyond death, consists in personal communion with Christ. The heart of the promise to the dying thief was this: 'You will be with me.' This is our blessed assurance, that to depart is 'to be with Christ' which is 'very far better.'"[5]

On which side of the cross are you?

From the side of Jesus Christ, one man may go to heaven and another to hell. On which side of the cross are you?

The Death of Our Lord (23:44-49)

Darkness covered the whole land from the sixth to the ninth hour, that is, from noon to 3 p.m. This was a sign to the nation of Israel. They had rejected the light, and now they would be denied light.

The veil of the temple was torn in two from the top to the bottom. This pictured the fact that through the death of the Lord Jesus Christ, a way of approach to God was opened to all who would come by faith (Heb. 10:20-22).

It was during these three hours of darkness that Jesus bore the penalty of our sins in His body on the tree. At the close of that time, He commended His spirit into the hands of God, His Father, and voluntarily yielded up His life. A Roman centurion was so overwhelmed by the scene that he glorified God saying, "Certainly this was a righteous Man!" The crowd was overcome by an awful sense of sorrow and foreboding. Some of Jesus' faithful followers, including women from Galilee, stood off in the shadows, watching this most crucial scene in the history of the world.

Burial of Christ's Body by Joseph (23:50-56)

Up to this time, Joseph had been a secret disciple of the Lord Jesus. Although a member of the Sanhedrin, yet he did not agree with their verdict in the case of Jesus. Joseph now went boldly to Pilate and asked if he might have the privilege of removing the body of the Lord Jesus from the cross and giving it a proper burial. (It was between 3 and 6 p.m.) Permission was granted, and Joseph promptly embalmed the body (aided by Nicodemus, another believing Pharisee, see John 19:39) and laid it in a tomb which he had ordered to be carved out of solid stone and which had never been used up to this time. This happened on Friday, the day of the preparation. When it says in verse 54 that the Sabbath drew on or was beginning to dawn we must remember that the Jewish Sabbath began on Friday at sunset.

The faithful women from Galilee followed Joseph as he took the body to the tomb and laid it inside. Then they went back to prepare spices and ointments so that they could return and further embalm the body of the one they loved.

In burying the body of Jesus, Joseph also buried himself, in a sense. That act separated him forever from the nation that crucified the Lord of life and glory. He would never be a part of the Jewish world again, but would live in moral separation from it and testify against it.

The Lord Is Risen! (24:1-12)

On Saturday the women rested, in obedience to the commandment concerning the Sabbath. Then at early dawn on Sunday morning they made their way to the tomb, carrying spices that they had prepared for the body of Jesus. But how did they expect to get to His body? Did they not know that a huge stone had been rolled against the mouth of the tomb? We are not told the answer. All we know is that they loved Him dearly, and love is often forgetful of difficulties in order to reach its object.

When they arrived they found the stone had been rolled away from the mouth of the tomb. As soon as they entered, they saw that the body of Jesus was missing. It is not difficult to imagine their perplexity. While they were still trying to reason it out, two angelic beings (see John 20:12), in dazzling clothes, appeared and assured them that Jesus was alive; it was pointless to search for Him in the tomb. He had risen, as He promised when they were in Galilee. Had He not foretold them that the Son of Man had to be turned over to wicked men and be slain, and that on the third day He would rise again? (Luke 9:22; 18:33). Then it all came back to them. They returned hurriedly to the city and told the news to the eleven disciples. Among those first heralds of the resurrection were Mary Magdalene, Joanna, and Mary the mother of James.

> Love is often forgetful of difficulties in order to reach its object.

The disciples didn't believe them at all. Incredible! Fantastic! That is what they thought—until Peter made a personal visit to the tomb and saw the linen clothes lying there by themselves. These were the clothes that had been tightly wound around the body. We are not told whether they were unwound, or still in the shape of the body, but we are safe in presuming the latter. It appears that the Lord may have left the grave-clothes as if they had been a cocoon. The fact that the grave-clothes were left behind shows that the body was not stolen; thieves probably would not have taken time to remove the coverings. Peter returned to his house, still trying to solve the mystery. What did it all mean?

The Road to Emmaus (24:13-35)

One of the two Emmaus disciples was a man named Cleopas; we do not know the identity of the other. It may have been his wife. All we can be sure of is that it was not one of the original eleven disciples (see v. 33).

The two were sadly rehearsing the death and burial of the Lord as they returned from Jerusalem to Emmaus, a journey of about seven and a half miles. As they proceeded, a stranger came alongside them; it was the risen Lord but they did not recognize Him. He asked them what they had been talking about. Cleopas expressed surprise that even a stranger in Jerusalem could have been unaware of what had happened. Jesus drew them out further with the question, "What things?" Cleopas answered, "The things concerning Jesus of Nazareth, who was a Prophet mighty in deed and word before God and all the people, and how the chief priests and our rulers delivered Him to be condemned to death, and crucified Him. But we were hoping that it was He who was going to redeem Israel. Indeed, besides all this, today is the third day since these things happened. Yes, and certain women of our company, who arrived at the tomb early, astonished us. When they did not find His body, they came saying that they had also seen a vision of angels who said He was alive."

Jesus then lovingly chided them for not realizing that this was exactly the pathway that the prophets of the Old Testament had foretold for the Messiah. First, He must suffer, then He would be glorified. Beginning at Genesis and continuing through the books of the Old Testament, the Lord reviewed all the passages that referred to Himself, the Messiah. It was a wonderful Bible study, and we would love to have been with Him then. But we have the same Old Testament Scriptures, and we have the Holy Spirit to teach us, so we too can discover in all the Scriptures the things concerning Himself.

——————— ❧ ———————

We too can discover in the Scriptures the things concerning Himself.

——————— ❧ ———————

By now the disciples were nearing their home. They invited their fellow-traveler to spend the night with them. At first, He courteously acted as if He were going to continue His journey; He would not force an entry. But they prevailed on Him to stay with them, and how richly they were rewarded! When they sat down for the evening meal, the Guest took the place of Host. "The frugal meal became a sacrament, and the home became a House of God. That's what Christ does wherever He goes. They who entertain Him will be well entertained. The two had opened to Him their home, and now He opens their eyes" (Daily Notes). As He broke the bread and passed it to them, they recognized Him for the first time. Had they seen the print of the nails in His hands? We only know that their eyes had been miraculously opened to recognize Him. As soon as this happened, He vanished.

Then they retraced the day's journey. No wonder their hearts had burned within them while He talked with them and explained the Scriptures. Their Teacher and Companion had been the risen Lord Jesus Christ. Instead of spending the night at Emmaus, they raced back to Jerusalem where they found "the eleven" and others assembled together. "The eleven" here is a general term to indicate the original band of the disciples, excluding Judas. Actually not all eleven were present, as we learn from John 20:24, but the term "eleven" is used in a collective sense.

Before the Emmaus disciples could share their joyful news, the Jerusalem disciples jubilantly announced that the Lord had really risen and had appeared to Simon (Peter). Then it was the turn of the two from Emmaus to say, "They told about the things that had happened on the road, and how He was known to them in the breaking of bread."

Jesus Appears to Disciples in Jerusalem (24:36-43)

The resurrection body of the Lord Jesus was a literal, tangible body of flesh and bones. It was the same body that had been buried, yet it was changed in that it was no longer subject to death. With this glorified body, Jesus could enter a room when the doors were closed. This is what He did on that first Sunday night. The disciples looked up and saw Him, then heard Him say, "Peace to you." They were seized with panic, thinking it was a ghost. Only when He showed them the marks of His passion in His hands and in His feet did they begin to understand. Even then, it was almost too good to be true. Then in order to show them it was really Jesus Himself, He ate broiled fish and a piece of honeycomb.

> The resurrection body of the Lord Jesus was a literal, tangible body of flesh and bones.

Jesus Sends Them Forth (24:44-49)

These verses may be a summary of Christ's teaching between His resurrection and His ascension. He explained that His resurrection was the fulfillment of His own words to them. Had He not told them that all the Old Testament prophecies concerning Him had to be fulfilled? The law of Moses, the prophets, and the Psalms were the three main divisions of the Old Testament. Taken together, they signify the entire Old Testament.

What was the burden of the Old Testament prophecies concerning Christ? They were that He should suffer (Ps. 22:1-21; Isa. 53:1-9) that He should rise again from the dead the third day (Ps. 16:10; Jonah 1:17; Hosea 6:2) and that repentance and remission of sins should be preached in His name unto all the nations, beginning from Jerusalem. Jesus opened their understanding to comprehend all these Scriptures. Indeed, this seems to be a chapter of opened things. There is the opened tomb (v. 12), the opened home (v. 29), the opened eyes (v. 31), the opened Scriptures (v. 32), the opened lips (v. 35), the opened understanding (v. 45) and the opened heavens (v. 51).

The disciples were witnesses of the resurrection. They must go forth as heralds of the glorious message. But first they must wait for the promise of the Father, that is, for the coming of the Holy Spirit at Pentecost. Then they would be clothed with divine power to bear witness to the risen Christ. The Holy Spirit was promised by the Father in such Old Testament passages as Isaiah 44:3; Joel 2:28; Ezekiel 36:27.

Christ Ascends to Heaven (24:50-53)

The ascension of Christ took place forty days after His resurrection. He took His disciples to Bethany, on the eastern side of the Mount of Olives. There He lifted up His hands and blessed them. While doing so, He was taken up into heaven. They bowed in worship, and then hastened back to Jerusalem with the news. For the next ten days, they spent much time at the temple, praising and blessing God. Luke's gospel opened with devout believers at the temple, praying for the long-expected Messiah. It closes at the same place with devout believers blessing and praising God for answered prayer and for accomplished redemption. It is a lovely climax to what Renan called the most beautiful book in the world.

[1] James S. Stewart, *op. cit.*, p. 161.
[2] James S. Stewart, *op. cit.*, p. 166.
[3] G. Campbell Morgan, *op. cit.*, p. 269.
[4] James S. Stewart, *op. cit.*, p. 168.
[5] Charles R. Erdman, *op. cit.*, pp. 217, 218.

THE
GOSPEL OF
LUKE

EXAM BOOKLET
AK '11   (2 UNITS)   LK

STUDENT NAME (PLEASE PRINT)

ADDRESS

CITY, STATE, ZIP

COURSE GRADE: _____

INSTRUCTOR

Exam developed by Emmaus Correspondence School, founded in 1942.

A NOTE ON THE EXAMS

The exams are designed to check your knowledge of the course material and the Scriptures. After you have studied a chapter, review the exam questions for that lesson. If you have difficulty in answering the questions, re-read the material. If questions contain a Scripture reference, you may use your Bible to help you answer them. If your instructor has provided a single page Answer Sheet, record your answer on that sheet. This exam contains the following types of questions:

MULTIPLE CHOICE

You will be asked to write in the letter of the correct answer at the space on the right. Here is an example:

The color of grass is

A.	blue	C.	yellow	
B.	green	D.	orange	**B**

WHAT DO YOU SAY?

Questions headed this way are designed to help you express your ideas and feelings. You may freely state your own opinions in answer to such questions.

RETURNING THE EXAM

See the back of this exam booklet for instructions on returning your exam for grading.

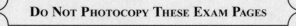
DO NOT PHOTOCOPY THESE EXAM PAGES

First Printed 1968 (AK '68), 1 UNIT
Revised 1974 (AK '74), 1 UNIT
Revised 2005 (AK '05), 1 UNIT
Reprinted 2008 (AK '05), 1 UNIT
Revised 2011 (AK '11), 2 UNITS
Reprinted 2014, 2020 (AK '11), 2 UNITS

ISBN 978-0-940293-29-8

Code: LK

Printed in the United States of America

CHAPTER 1 EXAM

THE BIRTH AND BOYHOOD OF JESUS

_____
EXAM GRADE

Before starting this exam, write your name and address on the front of this Exam Booklet.

Directions: Read each question carefully and write the letter of the correct answer in the blank space on the right. Use the separate answer sheet if provided.

1. Luke's emphasis is on Jesus as
   A. the Son of God   C. the Servant of Jehovah
   B. the Son of Man   D. the King of Israel   _____

2. In Luke's gospel, the topic of discipleship
   A. is limited to what Christ taught His followers
   B. is demonstrated only by Christ's example
   C. is evident in Christ's life as well as His teaching
   D. is not to be found at all   _____

3. In writing his gospel, Luke
   A. relied only on his firsthand knowledge of the facts
   B. depended totally on human documents
   C. was inspired of the Holy Spirit so had no need of human documents
   D. used oral and written sources but was still guided by the Holy Spirit   _____

4. The first important matter recorded in Luke's gospel is
   A. the genealogy of the Lord Jesus
   B. the announcement of the birth of John the Baptist
   C. the announcement to the Virgin Mary of the birth of Jesus
   D. the visit of the wise men to Bethlehem   _____

5. When Mary wanted to know how she could become the mother of Israel's Messiah she was told that
   A. it would be by means of a miraculous virgin birth
   B. she would have to marry Joseph first
   C. she must have more faith in God
   D. her cousin Elizabeth would tell her   _____

6. When John the Baptist was named after his birth

    A. Jesus was already six months old
    B. his father became dumb
    C. Zacharias burst into an inspired hymn of praise to God
    D. Elizabeth sang the Magnificat   _____

7. How were the shepherds told they would be able to recognize the promised Messiah?

    A. He'd be performing miracles
    B. King Herod would be there worshiping Him
    C. The wise men would be giving Him gifts
    D. He'd be lying in an animal manger   _____

8. The second of the three rituals performed at the time of Christ's birth was

    A. the circumcision of Jesus
    B. the baptism of Jesus
    C. the purification of Mary
    D. the presentation of Jesus in the temple   _____

9. Several songs were sung at the occasion of Christ's birth. Who sang about the distress that would pierce Mary's soul?

    A. The angels   C. Zacharias
    B. Mary herself   D. Simeon   _____

10. The Lord Jesus was taken by Joseph and Mary to Jerusalem when He was twelve years old because

    A. Jesus wanted to see the temple
    B. He needed further education
    C. at the age of twelve a Jewish boy becomes a man
    D. it was time for Israel to acknowledge her Messiah   _____

WHAT DO YOU SAY?

What *spiritual* lesson drawn in the course from Luke 1 and 2 has impressed you most?

_____

_____

_____

_____

CHAPTER 2 EXAM

JESUS BEGINS HIS MINISTRY

EXAM GRADE
_____

Write the letter of the correct answer in the blank space on the right.
Use the separate answer sheet if provided.

1. John the Baptist is described as
   - A. "a mighty rushing wind"
   - B. "a voice crying in the wilderness"
   - C. "a reed shaken in the breeze"
   - D. "the hammer of God"   _____

2. John's advice to the soldiers who responded to his teaching was
   - A. avoid extortion, slander, and discontent
   - B. resign from the army or, if that is not possible, desert
   - C. refuse to kill anyone, even in war
   - D. study your profession and seek rapid promotion   _____

3. The "baptism of fire" spoken of by John was a direct reference to
   - A. the Lord's death
   - B. his own martyrdom
   - C. baptism of the Spirit at Pentecost
   - D. the judgment of the unsaved   _____

4. The genealogy of the Lord Jesus as found in Luke's gospel
   - A. completely contradicts the genealogy found in Matthew's gospel
   - B. gives Christ's ancestry back to David only
   - C. gives Christ's ancestry through Mary
   - D. gives Christ's claim to the throne of Israel through Solomon   _____

5. During the temptation in the wilderness, the Lord Jesus
   - A. refused to even listen to what Satan had to say
   - B. entered into a philosophical discussion with Satan
   - C. fled from the scene of the temptation
   - D. silenced Satan with three quotations from the book of Deuteronomy   _____

6. When the devil quoted Scripture to the Lord Jesus he

    A. quoted from Psalm 91
    B. quoted the passage in its full context
    C. quoted the passage out of context
    D. did so to prove that Scriptures are not inspired   _____

7. Examine the following quotation from Luke 4:13-14 "Now when the devil had ended every temptation, he departed from Him until an opportune time. Then Jesus returned in the power of the Spirit to Galilee." This quotation

    A. is inaccurate
    B. takes us to the next chronological event in the Lord's life
    C. skips over about a year's ministry in Judea
    D. is missing from most of the earlier manuscripts of Luke's gospel   _____

8. Why did the Lord stop reading from Isaiah 61:1-2 in the middle of a sentence? Because He

    A. did not agree with the prophet's next statement
    B. was interrupted by the angry voices of the people to whom He was reading
    C. wished to create a sensation in the synagogue
    D. knew He would not fulfill the remaining part of the sentence at His first coming   _____

9. As a result of giving examples of Gentiles who responded to God's Old Testament prophets, the people of Nazareth

    A. fell down and worshiped Jesus
    B. asked Jesus to teach them more
    C. went to John to be baptized
    D. tried to kill Jesus   _____

10. When Jesus healed people

    A. He asked them first how much faith they had
    B. the symptoms of illness gradually disappeared
    C. the cure was immediate and complete
    D. He asked to be paid for His services   _____

WHAT DO YOU SAY?

The Lord Jesus used Scripture when He was tempted. What do you learn from this?

_____

_____

_____

_____

CHAPTER 3 EXAM

JESUS CALLS HIS DISCIPLES

_____
EXAM GRADE

Write the letter of the correct answer in the blank space on the right.
Use the separate answer sheet if provided.

1. After the miraculous catch of fish,
    A. the disciples were able to feed the five thousand
    B. the Lord was hailed by the multitude as the true King of
        the Jews
    C. the Lord challenged the disciples to follow Him and
        catch men
    D. Jesus left Galilee for the last time   C

2. When the Lord healed the man who was "full of leprosy," He
    A. sent the cleansed leper to the priests as a testimony to
        them
    B. told the leper to tell all his friends about the miracle that
        had happened to him
    C. was besieged by lepers coming to be healed
    D. was congratulated by the priests   A

3. Levi (Matthew) accomplished which of the following great
    ministries for God? He
    A. evangelized India
    B. was instrumental in the conversion of the apostle Paul
    C. founded the Christian church
    D. wrote the first of the four gospels   D

4. The parable of the two garments teaches that
    A. Christianity has been tacked on to Judaism
    B. mixing law and grace spoils both
    C. the Christian faith is really very old and worn
    D. Christianity includes Judaism   B

5. When the Pharisees criticized Christ because His disciples
    picked grain on the Sabbath, He
    A. told the disciples not to do it again
    B. responded with a parable about sowing seed
    C. claimed to be Lord of the Sabbath
    D. agreed that the disciples had broken the law   C

Luke 6:12

6. Which of the following was *NOT* a disciple of the Lord Jesus?

   A. James, the son of Zebedee   C. Simon, the Zealot
   B. James, the son of Alphaeus   D. John the Baptist   *D*

7. When Jesus said "Blessed are you poor" He meant

   A. poverty is a blessed condition
   B. poverty in spirit is a blessed state
   C. those who choose to be poor to follow Him are blessed
   D. God will bless the poor eventually with riches   *B*

8. In the great sermon of Luke 6:20-49, we find that

   A. we should seek the approval of others
   B. we should love our enemies
   C. when persecuted, we have a reason to be discouraged
   D. following Christ will result in happiness and riches   *B*

9. The Bible teaches "forgive and you will be forgiven" and
   also that we are freely forgiven when we accept Christ.
   These two statements   *?*

   A. are completely contradictory
   B. need not be taken literally
   C. speak of different types of forgiveness
   D. are not in the original text of the Bible   *(?) A*

10. Which of the following does Jesus call "wise"? The man who

    A. is poor, hungry, and persecuted for Christ's sake
    B. invests his money for his old age
    C. builds his life on what he thinks best
    D. follows the principles of the world   *A*

WHAT DO YOU SAY?

Which of the sayings of Luke 6:20-49 has made the biggest impression on
you? Explain how or why.

_____

_____

_____

_____

EXAM BOOKLET

CHAPTER 4 EXAM

MIRACLES AND PARABLES

_____
EXAM GRADE

Write the letter of the correct answer in the blank space on the right.
Use the separate answer sheet if provided.

1. When the centurion came to Christ to plead on behalf of his servant he said,
   A. "I am a Roman centurion"
   B. "I am willing to pay anything"
   C. "I am not worthy"
   D. "I am not going to command but beg"
   _____

2. At Nain, the Lord Jesus
   A. healed the servant of a centurion
   B. preached in the synagogue
   C. raised a young man to life
   D. turned water into wine
   _____

3. When the Lord said of John the Baptist that there was no greater prophet than he, the inference is that
   A. John was virgin born as well
   B. no one has ever had such integrity of character as did John
   C. no one has ever been the subject of such extensive prophecy as was John
   D. his greatness was connected with his being the Messiah's forerunner
   _____

4. Jesus was criticized in the house of Simon the Pharisee because He
   A. did not wash his hands before eating
   B. allowed a sinful woman to minister to Him
   C. healed a paralyzed man on the Sabbath day
   D. told the Jews to pay their taxes to the Roman government
   _____

5. The women mentioned in Luke 8:1-3 (Mary Magdalene, Joanna, Susanna) are examples to us how Jesus was blessed in His life with
   A. generous practical help
   B. fellow teachers
   C. medical help
   D. people to organize His busy schedule   _____

6. Today the kingdom of God is
   A. present in all its reality in the church
   B. in its mystery form
   C. rejected by the Gentiles but accepted by the Jews
   D. dormant until the second coming of Christ   _____

7. In the parable of the sower, the seed, and the soil, the birds represented
   A. believers   C. the devil
   B. angels of heaven   D. unbelievers   _____

8. After Jesus calmed the storm on the lake, He said to His disciples,
   A. "I'm sorry I fell asleep"
   B. "Why didn't you wake Me earlier?"
   C. "Where is your faith?"
   D. "You are such cowards"   _____

9. The healing of the man called Legion
   A. shows that Christ did not like pigs
   B. reveals Jesus' power over vast demonic forces
   C. should not be taught to children
   D. resulted in the conversion of the whole area   _____

10. As Jesus was on His way to the house of Jairus, He
    A. stopped to rebuke the money changers in the temple
    B. brushed aside all those who would get in His way
    C. was interrupted by a sick woman
    D. took time to teach the crowd two new parables   _____

EXAM BOOKLET

WHAT DO YOU SAY?

How would you evaluate the soil of your own soul?

_____

_____

_____

_____

CHAPTER 5 EXAM

TRAINING THE DISCIPLES

Write the letter of the correct answer in the blank space on the right.
Use the separate answer sheet if provided.

1. Herod's conscience was troubled because he had
   A. murdered his father in order to usurp his throne
   B. had John the Baptist beheaded
   C. neglected to finish building the temple in Jerusalem
   D. decided to crucify Jesus

2. The "watershed" of Jesus' dealings with His disciples came when
   A. John the Baptist was imprisoned
   B. Peter walked on the water
   C. Peter confessed Him as the Christ of God
   D. they all forsook Him and fled

3. Which of the following are deterrents against a life of discipleship?
   A. The desire to save our lives by self-indulgence
   B. The desire to acquire worldly wealth
   C. The fear of shame
   D. All the above

4. When Jesus was transfigured, Moses and Elijah spoke with Him about
   A. His miraculous virgin birth
   B. His forthcoming exodus
   C. His coming kingdom
   D. His miracles

5. When Jesus came down from the Mount, He was met by
   A. a demoniac situation
   B. a crowd crying "Hosanna!"
   C. a deputation of John the Baptist's disciples
   D. a man born blind

EXAM BOOKLET

6. To illustrate His lesson on humility, Jesus used
   A. a worm
   C. a wayside flower
   B. a child
   D. a marking in the dust   _____

7. Two of the three would-be disciples used an identical phrase when stating the conditional type of obedience they were willing to give. Both implied,
   A. "When I can"
   C. "Me first"
   B. "If possible"
   D. "When I retire"   _____

8. The thought behind Jesus' sending His disciples out in two's seems to be that of
   A. competent testimony
   B. mutual protection
   C. continual surveillance
   D. personal encouragement   _____

9. The Lord pronounced His verdict of displeasure on
   A. Chorazin, Bethsaida, and Capernaum
   B. Tyre, Sidon, and Nineveh
   C. Egypt, Babylon, and Rome
   D. Nazareth, Bethlehem, and Samaria   _____

10. The story of the Good Samaritan was prompted by a question asked of Jesus by
   A. a tax collector
   C. a Pharisee
   B. a centurion
   D. a lawyer   _____

WHAT DO YOU SAY?

To "take up the cross" means to deliberately choose the kind of life Christ lived. Describe this kind of life.

_____

_____

_____

_____

CHAPTER 6 EXAM

TEACHING OF JESUS

Write the letter of the correct answer in the blank space on the right.
Use the separate answer sheet if provided.

1. Which of the following was unknown to Old Testament believers?
   A. Prayer for physical well-being
   B. Prayer to God as Father
   C. Prayer for cleansing from sin
   D. Prayer as a personal exercise

2. When Jesus cast out a demon which had caused a person to be dumb, He was
   A. accused of being in league with the prince of demons
   B. willing to prove that His power was divine and not satanic in origin
   C. acclaimed by the multitudes as Israel's true Messiah
   D. angry at the reaction to the miracle

3. In response to the woman who cried out, "Blessed is the womb that bore You," Jesus conveyed that
   A. Mary was blessed above all other women
   B. Mary was no more blessed than anyone else
   C. His mother should be appealed to at all times
   D. even Mary was more blessed in believing on Christ and in following Him than she was in being His mother

4. In calling His generation "an evil generation," the Lord made two appeals to history.
   A. To the Queen of Sheba and to the Ninevites
   B. To the Edomites and to the Amalekites
   C. To Daniel and to the people of Tyre
   D. To the Egyptians and to the Canaanites

5. The Pharisee who invited Jesus to supper was shocked at Him because He
   A. omitted to give thanks for the food
   B. failed to wash (bathe) before eating
   C. washed His disciples' feet
   D. ate with His fingers

6. Jesus told His disciples to beware of the leaven of the Pharisees and explained that leaven was a symbol of
   A. ritualism   C. hypocrisy
   B. immorality   D. unbelief

7. Those who confess Christ now will be
   A. praised of men
   B. pardoned for their sins
   C. welcomed by those in high places
   D. confessed by Christ before the angels

8. In the view of the author, which of the Ten Commandments (in Exodus 20) do men break with hardly a thought?
   A. the sixth   C. the eighth
   B. the seventh   D. the tenth

9. When Jesus said, "Let your waist be girded and your lamps burning," (12:35) He was speaking in the light of
   A. coming persecution   C. the exodus from Egypt
   B. His return   D. His resurrection

10. The Lord's statement about man's ability to predict the weather and his blindness about the significance of the times was addressed specifically to
    A. the Lord's people in all ages
    B. only Peter, James, and John
    C. the disciples alone
    D. the multitude

WHAT DO YOU SAY?

What is your reaction to the teaching on discipleship in this section of the gospel?

_____

_____

_____

_____

CHAPTER 7 EXAM

WARNINGS

EXAM GRADE

*Write the letter of the correct answer in the blank space on the right.
Use the separate answer sheet if provided.*

1. The massacre of some Galileans by Pilate
   A. led some to assume that the victims must have deserved it
   B. was a clear-cut case of divine retribution for unusual sin
   C. took place at the tower of Siloam
   D. led the Lord to leave Judea

2. The fig tree in the Lord's parable represented
   A. Israel   C. Rome
   B. the church   D. Jerusalem

3. In the Lord's parable of the fig tree, the vinedresser who knew that the order to "cut it down" had been issued represents
   A. the godly remnant in Israel   C. the Holy Spirit
   B. the church   D. the Lord Jesus

4. The Lord Jesus reproved the hypocrisy of
   A. Simon Peter
   B. the ruler of the synagogue
   C. the Samaritans
   D. Thomas

5. Which two parables picture the growth of Christendom?
   A. The prodigal son and the elder brother
   B. The good Samaritan and the rich fool
   C. The mustard seed and the leaven
   D. The lost sheep and the talents

6. Who, *specifically*, will see Abraham, Isaac, and Jacob and all the prophets in the kingdom of God while they themselves are excluded?
   A. The unbelieving Israelites   C. The fallen angels
   B. The Gentiles   D. Satan

7. Who did the Lord Jesus call a she-fox?

    A. Pilate   C. Herod

    B. Judas   D. Caiaphas   _____

8. The Jews condemned the Lord Jesus for

    A. cleansing the temple on the Sabbath

    B. rescuing an animal trapped in a pit on the Sabbath

    C. healing a man on the Sabbath

    D. preaching in the synagogue on the Sabbath   _____

9. In the Lord's parable, the invitation to the supper was rejected by

    A. a person who put material things first

    B. a person who put his job first

    C. a person who put his family ties first

    D. all the above   _____

10. The Lord's illustration about a king going to war against a bigger rival was given in connection with His teaching on

    A. the second coming   C. loving one's neighbor

    B. discipleship   D. persecution   _____

WHAT DO YOU SAY?

What can we learn about the "cost" of following Christ from this lesson? What are the benefits of following Christ?

_____

_____

_____

_____

CHAPTER 8 EXAM

GROWING OPPOSITION

_____
EXAM GRADE

Write the letter of the correct answer in the blank space on the right.
Use the separate answer sheet if provided.

1. The parables of the lost sheep, the lost coin, and the lost son
   were
   A. aimed at the scribes and Pharisees
   B. told to the disciples in private in the upper room
   C. intended to show that the tax-collectors and sinners
      were further from God than the religious leaders
   D. spoken after the tax-collectors and sinners had left
      the Lord   _____

2. In the parable of the lost sheep, the ninety-nine represented
   A. those who don't need to repent
   B. those who don't think they need to repent
   C. those who have already repented
   D. those who are in heaven rejoicing   _____

3. The prodigal son made two requests. Which was his coming
   home request? (see Luke 15:19)
   A. "Father, give me . . ."   C. "Father, make me . . ."
   B. "Father, help me . . ."   D. "Father, send me . . ."   _____

4. Why is the parable of the unjust steward one of the most
   difficult in the gospel? Because
   A. it is not found in the best manuscripts of Luke's gospel
   B. it degrades manual labor
   C. it applauds violence
   D. it seems to commend dishonesty   _____

5. From the parable of the unjust steward we should learn
   A. dishonesty is sometimes acceptable
   B. a believer always acts more wisely than an unbeliever
   C. material possessions are evil
   D. to sacrifice present gain for future reward   _____

6. Which of the following is meant by the phrase "unrighteous mammon"?

   A. wicked men   C. big business
   B. money   D. religious hypocrites   _____

7. The Lord's teaching on wealth prompted the Pharisees to

   A. increase their donations to the temple
   B. give more money to the poor
   C. envy the disciples their poor and humble condition in life
   D. sneer at the Lord   _____

8. The rich man was condemned to Hades because

   A. he was rich
   B. his treatment of Lazarus proved his lack of saving faith
   C. he was not a Jew
   D. his brothers forgot to pray for him   _____

9. In the Old Testament, riches were a sign of God's blessing. In the New Testament they are

   A. also a sign of God's blessing
   B. a curse
   C. a test of faithfulness in stewardship
   D. a means of grace   _____

10. When the rich man pleaded that his brothers would believe if someone came to them from the dead, Abraham

   A. agreed with him
   B. promised to send Lazarus to them
   C. told him that failure to heed God's Word is final
   D. referred the rich man to the resurrection of Christ   _____

WHAT DO YOU SAY?

What lesson have you learned for your own life from this lesson with respect to money or wealth?

_____

_____

_____

_____

EXAM BOOKLET

CHAPTER 9 EXAM

ATTITUDES

<u>_____</u>
EXAM GRADE

Write the letter of the correct answer in the blank space on the right.
Use the separate answer sheet if provided.

1. The Lord Jesus indicated that to stumble a little one (a child or a young believer) is
   A. not very serious
   B. to become guilty of a very serious offense indeed
   C. an offense against man but not against God
   D. the unpardonable sin   _____

2. The real purpose of rebukes and other disciplinary action is to
   A. humiliate the offender
   B. expose the offender
   C. excommunicate the offender
   D. restore the offender to fellowship   _____

3. The sin of ingratitude was evident
   A. in the parable of the Good Samaritan
   B. by the cleansed Jewish lepers
   C. by the master of the unprofitable servant
   D. at the marriage in Cana   _____

4. According to the Lord Jesus, the days immediately prior to His coming to reign would be
   A. prosperous and peaceful
   B. marked by a worldwide turning to Christianity
   C. materialistic and godless
   D. all the above   _____

5. Lot's wife
   A. was the only person saved when Sodom was destroyed
   B. proves that people have a second chance to be saved even after rejecting the gospel
   C. was overtaken by judgment because her heart was still in Sodom
   D. refused to leave Sodom and perished in its flames   _____

6. The unrighteous judge was moved to action by the persistence of

   A. a praying widow   C. a praying tax-collector
   B. a praying Pharisee   D. a praying beggar   _____

7. Which of the following prayed "with himself"?

   A. Simon Peter   C. John the Baptist
   B. The Pharisee   D. The Good Samaritan   _____

8. Of whom was the Lord speaking when He said "of such is the kingdom of God"?

   A. The twelve apostles   C. The prophets
   B. The patriarchs   D. Little children   _____

9. The ruler who came to Christ wanting to know what to do to inherit eternal life

   A. found out he already possessed it
   B. was able to prove that he had kept the Ten Commandments
   C. became a disciple of the Lord Jesus
   D. was not prepared to do what was necessary to get it   _____

10. The blind beggar at Jericho

    A. did not know who Jesus was
    B. recognized Jesus to be the Messiah
    C. was sent to Siloam to be healed
    D. did not have enough faith to be healed   _____

What Do You Say?

Name one thing you have learned in this lesson that will help you be a better follower of Christ (and if possible, how).

_____

_____

_____

_____

EXAM BOOKLET

CHAPTER 10 EXAM

ON TO JERUSALEM

_____
EXAM GRADE

Write the letter of the correct answer in the blank space on the right. Use the separate answer sheet if provided.

1. One of the evidences of the genuineness of the conversion of Zacchaeus is seen in his
   A. ability to preach
   B. resignation from the Sanhedrin
   C. new attitude toward money
   D. regular attendance at the synagogue   _____

2. The expression "son of Abraham" denotes that
   A. Zacchaeus was a physical descendant of Abraham and no more
   B. Zacchaeus was a Gentile converted to Judaism
   C. Zacchaeus had married into a Jewish family
   D. Zacchaeus exercised the same kind of faith that Abraham did   _____

3. The chief point of the parable of the pounds is that
   A. the kingdom of God is within us
   B. there would be an interval between the two advents
   C. the gospel will ultimately triumph in the conversion of all mankind
   D. all men are sinners   _____

4. As the Lord rode in triumph into Jerusalem the people cried
   A. "Peace in heaven!"   C. "Glory be to God!"
   B. "Peace on earth!"   D. "Long live the King!"   _____

5. When weeping over Jerusalem, Jesus specifically had in mind the coming
   A. siege under Titus
   B. revolt under Bar Cochba
   C. Mohammedan rule over the city
   D. defilement of the city by the Antichrist   _____

6. The cleansing of the temple mentioned in Luke 19 is
   A. the only such cleansing by the Lord
   B. the second such cleansing by the Lord
   C. the third such cleansing by the Lord
   D. the same cleansing as that mentioned in John 2:14-17   _____

7. The Lord Jesus was attacked by His enemies three times in Luke 20. Which of the following is true? He was challenged along the line of authority
   A. only in religious matters
   B. only in domestic matters
   C. only in civil matters
   D. in religious, civil, and domestic matters   _____

8. The parable of the vineyard was
   A. intended to bring about the conversion of the tax-collectors and sinners
   B. told when Jesus was standing before Caiaphas
   C. an indictment of the chief priests and scribes
   D. actually a repetition of the parable found in Isaiah 5:1-7   _____

9. The Lord's famous dictum "Render to Caesar the things that are Caesar's and to God the things that are God's" was spoken in answer to
   A. a politically "loaded" question
   B. a sincere question put by those who desired to solve a knotty national problem
   C. a question which was currently being debated on the floor of the Sanhedrin in Jerusalem
   D. a question put to Christ by agents of Pilate, the Roman governor   _____

10. The question about a man marrying his brother's widow was
    A. asked by the Pharisees
    B. based on an established precept of the Mosaic law
    C. ignored by the Lord Jesus
    D. asked out of a genuine desire to understand the resurrection   _____

EXAM BOOKLET

WHAT DO YOU SAY?

What is your chief impression of the Lord Jesus as you have studied His handling of His enemies?

_____

_____

_____

_____

CHAPTER 11 EXAM

THE PLOT THICKENS

<u>EXAM GRADE</u>

Write the letter of the correct answer in the blank space on the right.
Use the separate answer sheet if provided.

1. The outline of future events in Luke 21
   A. is identical with the Olivet Discourse
   B. includes the prediction of the destruction of Jerusalem
   C. relates only to the tribulation at the end of the age
   D. details the history of the church   _____

2. The faith of Christ's disciples during these trying times would be proved to be genuine if they
   A. died as martyrs
   B. were instrumental in the salvation of many souls
   C. stayed in Jerusalem
   D. persevered and remained true to Christ   _____

3. Which of the following periods began with the Babylonian Captivity and will end with Christ's return to reign? The period called
   A. the times of the Gentiles
   B. the blessing of the Gentiles
   C. the rule of the Gentiles
   D. the fullness of the Gentiles   _____

4. The rebirth of the State of Israel was symbolically foretold by Jesus in His outline of future events in His reference to
   A. the vine   C. the olive tree
   B. the fig tree   D. the cedar tree   _____

5. The position taken by the author is that the phrase "this generation" in Luke 21 refers to
   A. the generation living while Jesus was on earth
   B. the generation which will be living in the end times
   C. the Jewish people during the period of their hostility to Christ
   D. the Gentiles in their age-long enmity toward the Jews _____

6. The mission of Peter and John into Jerusalem to find a man with a pitcher of water
   A. would not be hard, as usually the women carried water pots
   B. was hard because so many men would be seen carrying pitchers
   C. was only possible of accomplishment because of the further description given both of the man and the pitchers
   D. was easy as they both knew where they were going _____

7. The bread and wine used by Christ to inaugurate the Lord's Supper
   A. were turned into His literal body and blood
   B. were not turned into His literal body and blood then but now they are whenever the Lord's Supper is commemorated
   C. were used by the Lord in a symbolic way only
   D. marked the new feast as a revised form of the old Passover feast _____

8. The Lord addressed Peter as "Simon, Simon"
   A. every time He spoke to him
   B. six times altogether
   C. when Simon asked permission to walk on the water
   D. at the time the Lord warned Peter he would deny Him _____

9. How many different denials of the Lord by Peter are recorded in the gospels?
   A. one   C. six
   B. two   D. ten _____

10. Judas actually betrayed the Lord Jesus
   A. in the upper room
   B. in the garden of Gethsemane
   C. before Caiaphas
   D. before Pilate _____

What Do You Say?

What is it about the Lord Jesus in these chapters that prompts you to worship Him?

_____

_____

_____

_____

CHAPTER 12 EXAM

DEATH! RESURRECTION! GLORY!

EXAM GRADE

Write the letter of the correct answer in the blank space on the right. Use the separate answer sheet if provided.

1. On which of the following charges was the Lord Jesus arraigned at His civil trial?
   A. Subversion against Rome
   B. Forbidding Jews to pay Roman taxes
   C. Making Himself a king
   D. All the above

2. The Herod who had a part in the trial of Jesus was the Herod who
   A. massacred the babies of Bethlehem
   B. murdered John the Baptist
   C. tried the apostle Paul
   D. was called "Herod the Great"

3. Alexander and Rufus were
   A. forced to carry the cross for Christ
   B. Roman soldiers
   C. servants of the high priest
   D. sons of Simon of Cyrene

4. When describing the actual crucifixion, the Scripture
   A. uses great restraint
   B. gives all the gory details
   C. implies that the Jews, not the Romans, invented crucifixion
   D. describes what Christ was thinking on the cross

5. The one dying thief was saved because he
   A. was basically a good man
   B. had been baptized by John
   C. confessed his sinfulness and put his faith in Christ
   D. had a godly mother

6. The tearing of the veil in the temple
  A. took place at about 5 p.m.
  B. was done by the priests
  C. signified that Christ had, by dying, made access to God possible for all
  D. caused the Jews to abandon Judaism _____

7. The first ones to spread the news of Christ's resurrection were
  A. women
  B. Peter, James, and John
  C. the soldiers who had guarded the tomb
  D. Matthew, Mark, Luke, and John _____

8. On the Emmaus road, Jesus spoke to His two disciples of
  A. things foretold about Him in the Old Testament
  B. His second coming to earth
  C. the impending doom of Jerusalem
  D. the creation of His church _____

9. Jesus revealed Himself to the two disciples in the home at Emmaus by
  A. performing a miracle
  B. breaking bread
  C. telling them who He was
  D. writing His name on the sandy floor _____

10. The ascension of Christ into heaven took place
  A. forty days after His resurrection
  B. from the temple in Jerusalem
  C. when no one was around to see it
  D. on the day of Pentecost _____

WHAT DO YOU SAY?

What significance does the resurrection of Christ have for you?

_____
_____
_____
_____

EXAM BOOKLET

RETURNING THE EXAM BOOKLET FOR GRADING

- ✓ After completing the exam, check it carefully.
- ✓ Make sure you have followed the directions.
- ✓ Be sure you have written your correct name and address on all material you will send to the School.
- ✓ Return all the exams at one time instead of separating and mailing each individual exam.
- ✓ Return only this exam booklet, not the course book. If you have used the single page Answer Sheet, return only that sheet.
- ✓ Address the envelope correctly.
- ✓ Put the correct postage on the envelope.
- ✓ If you are studying this course through an Associate Instructor or associated ministry or organization, send the exams to the individual or organization from which you obtained the course. Otherwise, send them to the address below.

Pollo shirt

ECS Ministries
PO Box 1028
Dubuque, Iowa 52004-1028
(563) 585-2070
ecsorders@ecsministries.org
www.ecsministries.org